SO, WHY DIDN'T THEY TELL ME THAT IN CHURCH?

So, Why Didn't They Tell Me That In Church?

A Curious Layman Reveals Ten Things The Church Has Failed To Teach

S. Michael Owens

WestBow

P R E S S

A DIVISION OF THOMAS NELSON

WestBow Press books may be ordered through booksellers or by contacting:

WestBow Press
A Division of Thomas Nelson
1663 Liberty Drive
Bloomington, IN 47403
www.westbowpress.com
1-(866) 928-1240

Cover design and appendix graphics by Lisa Knight.
www.KurllyGurllDesigns.com

Any people depicted in stock imagery provided by Thinkstock are models, and such images are being used for illustrative purposes only.

Certain stock imagery © Thinkstock.

ISBN: 978-1-4497-9960-1 (sc)
ISBN: 978-1-4497-9962-5 (hc)
ISBN: 978-1-4497-9961-8 (e)

Library of Congress Control Number: 2013911533

Printed in the United States of America.

WestBow Press rev. date: 7/2/2013

CONTENTS

Briefly, Before We Start . . .

Capture their heart—and you will capture their mind.

One of the greatest theological statements I've ever heard was by a college student being interviewed on a campus in Atlanta. Todd Friel, host of Wretched Radio on Sirius, was talking to students on the sidewalks between classes, asking them questions that would encourage response and discussion.

One student apologized for his accent and explained that this was his first year away from his home in Korea. Todd asked if he considered himself to be a good person, to which he gave the normal answer, "Yes." Then, using a few questions that led the young man to realize that he had broken several of God's Ten Commandments (just as we all have), Todd asked if this concerned him. With further explanation he saw that he would be guilty on judgment day.

Then Todd asked him if he knew who Jesus was. His gentle and sheepish answer was, "No."

This short and considerate explanation came: "Jesus is God's Son. He came from Heaven two thousand years ago and lived on this earth, telling others about His Father and doing His work. Then He willingly allowed Himself to be brutally beaten and killed as He was nailed to a cross. This was His plan. He did this in order to pay the penalty for your sins—so that you could stand before God on judgment day with Jesus at your side."

The young Korean's response is something I will never forget. No explanations or excuses—a simple but heartfelt response. This is all he said:

"Jesus is very kind."

Each time I recall that young man's broken English stating this great truth, it impacts my soul.

Jesus has won my heart—now I want Him to have my mind.

One of the great Bible teachers of our day, R.C. Sproul, has stated the following: "It's a sin to bore people."

If Jesus has won your heart, my hope is that you will find the following pages exciting, illuminating, liberating—and never boring.

PREFACE

LET'S GET IT RIGHT

Our theology is important.

Our beliefs about God. His attributes and character. What He has revealed about Himself. This area of what we believe, our *theology,* is the most consequential subject we can grasp, and it deserves our serious attention.

Billy Graham stated that most people will spend weeks or months planning and anticipating a summer vacation, but rarely spend fifteen minutes in serious thought about eternity. Nothing will affect our lives more than our concept of God and His attributes, and our response to that understanding.

Getting our theology right is critical. If we want to think correctly, then we should desire to fine-tune our theology.

That's the purpose of this book. To help you evaluate your beliefs and see the potential need for a tune-up. And to hopefully assist you in acquiring a more accurate biblical view.

So, Why Didn't They Tell Me That in Church? tackles issues many of us have that surround the central issue of God's sovereignty. Many important principles flow from a clear appreciation of this essential truth. The subject of God's sovereignty in all things is something most Christians have only looked into casually. The book also tackles controversial—or perhaps not as controversial as they should be!—topics including tithing, the will of man, the nature of salvation, and a closer look at what the Bible tells us about the mortality of man accompanied with the language of destruction throughout Scripture. Particularly how these relate to our view of eternal punishment.

My hope is that you will take time to assess your current thoughts and ideas about each of these subjects. Open your Bible. Consider the points made in each of the following ten chapters. Then weigh, judge, and reason.

"The one who states his case first seems right,
until the other comes and examines him."
—Proverbs 18:17

For many of us, the views presented in this book will represent an alternate view—perhaps even a side of the issues that we were not aware existed. As this truth from Proverbs states, we need to be cautious about looking at only one side of an issue, even when we are not aware that there is an alternative view.

One important term in this book highlights the reason for studying these things. The term is *traditionalism*. In this book it can be defined as "beliefs that are founded in cultural acceptance."

The comment below, from Dr. J.I. Packer, summarizes the primary incentive of this book, which is to help us identify ideas that we generally accept because of traditionalism and consider the biblical strength—or lack thereof—for those notions.

Quotes Worth Requoting

"We do not start our Christian lives by working out our faith for ourselves; it is mediated to us by Christian tradition, in the form of sermons, books and established patterns of church life and fellowship. We read our Bibles in the light of what we have learned from these sources; *we approach Scripture with minds already formed by the mass of accepted opinions and viewpoints with which we have come into contact, in both the Church and the world.*

"It is easy to be unaware that it has happened; it is hard even to begin to realize how profoundly tradition in this sense has moulded us. But we are forbidden to become enslaved to human tradition, either secular or Christian, whether it be 'catholic' tradition, or 'critical' tradition, or 'ecumenical' tradition. We may never assume the complete rightness of our own established ways of thought and practice and excuse ourselves the duty of testing and reforming them by Scriptures."—J.I. Packer

"You cannot separate what a man believes from what he is. For this reason doctrine is vitally important. Certain people say ignorantly, 'I do not believe in doctrine; I believe in the Lord Jesus Christ; I am saved, I am a Christian, and nothing else matters'. To speak in that way is to court disaster, and for this reason, the *New Testament itself warns us against this very danger.* We are to guard ourselves against being 'tossed to and fro and carried about with every wind of doctrine', for if your doctrine goes astray your life will soon suffer as well.—So it behooves us to *study the doctrines in order that we may safeguard ourselves against certain erroneous and heretical teachings* that are as common in the world today as they were in the days of the early Church."—Martyn Lloyd-Jones

"Please don't disturb me with the facts,
I'm content in being lax.
I won't take time to think, you see;
If wrong, that's good enough for me."
—James E. Gibbons

"Yes, if truth is not undergirded by love, it makes the possessor of that truth obnoxious and the truth repulsive."—Ravi Zacharias

CHAPTER 1

GOD'S SOVEREIGNTY: WHAT DO YOU REALLY BELIEVE?

Goal & Purpose:
When asked if we believe in the sovereignty of God,
most of us will declare, "Yes." However, upon a closer
inspection, we might be surprised at what we truly
believe. Where we find ourselves on this crucial issue will
determine almost every theological position we hold.

"If God is not sovereign, then God is not God."
—R.C. Sproul

What is the sovereignty of God? It is His absolute power and dominion over His creatures and all His creation including every molecule, thought, and decision. It is not so much a single attribute as it is the culmination of all of God's characteristics, including His holiness, justice, love, grace, mercy, immutability, omnipotence, and omniscience.

Many Christians have stated that the greatest and most important change in their lives, other than their conversion to Christ, was seeing the sovereignty of God—seeing and understanding that God is sovereign in everything. Coming to terms with this truth is radical, and it will change the way you comprehend events in your life and the way you respond.

Those Christians who take that statement lightly might consider that they have not really come to terms with this truth. That's the way I was for most of my Christian life: acknowledging the sovereignty of God but not really thinking through the implications of that acknowledgment.

On the night of May 9, 2006, a tornado destroyed our home in Texas. Our youngest son, Colson, died in our home that night at the age of fourteen. His four brothers and sisters were grown and out of the house or at work.

God gave his mother and I an amazing comfort, a "peace that passes all understanding" The grief is real, and it will always be there as a sign of the love we have for our son, whom we miss every day.

One of the things I learned was that God doesn't *allow* tornadoes.

He *plans* them. In fact, He controls them better than a surgeon with a scalpel. However, that was not my view until a few years after the storm.

Determining Where We Stand

Most Christians profess to believe in God's omnipotence and omniscience—that He is *all*-powerful and *all*-knowing. However, a closer look will reveal that most people, including most Christians, don't really adhere to the "all" part. In reality, most of us think that God is not sovereign over cancer cells, car wrecks, or our personal decisions.

This is a crucial issue. Most of us never come face-to-face with this topic beyond a shallow discussion. Many just never make the effort to think through this key belief. But this crucial matter of God's sovereignty is much more pivotal than we might realize.

The following eight questions will help reveal whether you believe in a "limited omnipotence" of God or in His complete power and sovereignty.

1) Does God allow, and essentially cause, deadly car wrecks?
2) Does He cause and plan the death of hundreds or thousands of children in a tsunami?
3) Has God foreordained everything that happens?
4) If God is omnipotent, then He has the power to stop a cancer cell, a fire, a tornado, or even a divorce. If He holds the authority to stop a disastrous event, then is He responsible for it if He does not stop it?

5) Is there one event that will take place today outside of God's control?
6) Can our "free will" change or defy God's sovereign will?
7) Is there one dust particle or molecule in the universe outside of God's control?
8) Does anything ever happen outside of God's sovereign will?

If your answers to these eight questions were not a "yes" for 1 through 4 and a "no" for 5 through 8, then you might need to evaluate whether you really believe in the biblical teaching of the sovereignty of God.

My Conversion to God's Sovereignty

My son's death was a turning point in my understanding of God's sovereignty. I've come to realize that God must be in complete control of everything or nothing. *He is the author of life and death, and everything in between.* That conclusion is twofold: First, the Bible declares that God is sovereign over everything, omnipotent and omniscient—and that declaration is stated *several hundred times in Scripture.* Biblical Christianity recognizes the total sovereignty of God. Second, it makes no sense that God would be sovereign over some things but not others. Sovereign on Tuesdays but not Thursdays. The idea that He intervenes in our lives for some things and sits back watching as other things simply "occur" is illogical and does not fit what we know of God from the Scriptures.

I had to face the implications of this. The very fact that God sees everything and knows everything, coupled with His omnipotence, means that He has to be sovereignly in control of all. If He knew that a tornado was coming toward our home, and being *all*-powerful He did not stop it, then the tornado was His doing. In fact, if I really wanted to come to terms with God's sovereignty, I needed to go a step further and ask, "Did God kill my son?"

Before I give my answer to this important question, let me tell you about a radio broadcast I heard while God was helping me to understand this subject. The radio host had a pastor from Canada on his show by telephone. They were discussing the murder of the pastor's teenage daughter, who was killed in a park behind their home just a few days prior to the interview. After talking about the details of her death, they discussed God's place in the situation. Acknowledging that God is sovereign and in control of all things, the pastor revealed that God gives us every breath we have. He sustains us, and He plans our birth as well as our death.

When I heard this grieving father admit that God had killed his daughter, I was shocked. Many will deny that God kills anyone, much less a pastor's daughter walking through a park behind her home. This is hard. It's hard for us to admit. We want to acknowledge God's hand in the good things, but not the bad.

Yet, a truly biblical perspective will not allow us to take such a half-and-half approach. Who killed Jesus? We can blame it on the first-century Jews, the Romans, or even ourselves. The fact is, God planned and determined every detail of His Son's death. If you don't believe that, then you should do a serious study of God's Word on this all-important question.

In fact, it even pleased God to kill His Son. "Yet it was the LORD's will to crush Him and cause Him to suffer, and though the LORD makes His life an offering for sin, He will see His offspring and prolong His days, and the will of the LORD will prosper in His hand" (Isaiah 53:10).

If it was God's plan to send His own precious Son to die for our sins, how can I think that my child's life and death are beyond His sovereign and perfect plan? It gives God the glory He deserves when we agree with this truth in light of the horrors of disaster and death that each of us encounter. It is in such personal, life-and-death issues that the question of whether we really believe in God's sovereignty becomes apparent. If your response is, "No, God didn't kill your son," then you don't really believe in God's omnipotence, omniscience, and sovereignty. The fact is, God did kill my son that night. Without exception, He kills everyone. Everyone's birth and death line up with His sovereign plan. To deny this fact is to camouflage or disguise the truth.

Some Christians pick and choose the parts of Christian truth that suit their fancy, just like walking through a buffet line, choosing to believe what appeals to them and rejecting what is unappealing or difficult. However, the truths of the Bible are interconnected. We should think of the various doctrines presented to us in Scripture as the components in a well-tuned car engine rather than a selection of food on a cafeteria tray. The things we learn about God's character and the ways He works to redeem lost sinners and bring glory to Himself are finely tuned, and they all work in harmony. Taking the biblical truth of God's sovereign and controlling hand out of our theology is like removing the crankshaft from a car engine.

It is by our Father's desire and design that everyone who lives today is alive, and it is by His will that everyone who dies today will die. We can say that He lets them die, and that's certainly a more bearable way of expressing ourselves. But in our minds and deep in our hearts, it should be understood that God is in control of life and death.

Believe me, it was difficult the first time I admitted with my own lips that God had killed my son. However, I discovered that doing so enabled me to give God the glory for anything—and everything—that happens. When we finally admit that He is sovereign over every molecule and event, good or bad, then we can relax and not worry. More importantly, we can recognize that He is worthy of our adoration and worship.

A Deep Impact

The ramifications of whether we really believe God is 100 percent omnipotent—sovereign in everything—are far-reaching. Understanding this foundational precept will have an influence on every facet of our belief system.

Maintaining faith in a "god" who is not sovereignly in control of every detail of this universe is actually a form of idolatry. Why? A simple, abbreviated examination of Scripture makes it very clear that God is in control of all things. (See appendix A for a list of Bible verses declaring this truth.) If we hold to the idea that God is not *all-knowing and all-powerful and therefore entirely sovereign over all things,* then we are designing our own god. Designing a god to suit our own ideas is idolatry, not biblical Christianity.

Many Christians are inadvertently guilty of practicing a form of idolatry. They are worshiping a god of their own imaginations, or a god who has been presented to them by culture and traditionalism. Despite the fact that they might be surrounded by Bibles and good teachers, the god they are clinging to is not the God presented in the pages of Genesis through Revelation. True Christianity hinges on belief in God as He is described in His Word.

It's been said that if you sleep in the garage, that doesn't make you a car. The same is true of our faith: if you carry a Bible and go to church, that doesn't make you a biblical Christian. We need to be opening God's Word, studying it, believing what it clearly teaches about God's character and who He is, not who we want Him to be. This is paramount. If we desire to be worshipers of the true God—revealed in His Word—then we need to rely on His written and special revelation. God's sovereignty over every aspect and detail of our lives is a truth that radiates from virtually every page.

How Can We Know God's Attributes?

The foundation of our understanding of Scripture is knowing the nature of God. And the only dependable source for knowing about Him is His complete and sufficient Word, the Bible. All other sources are risky. A desire for truth, while admirable, is not the key to success. We can desire truth while being sincere—and at the same time we can find ourselves sincerely wrong. Outside of God's general revelation in nature, which Paul speaks about in Romans 1:18, the sixty-six books of the Bible are the *only* revelation God has given for a reliable understanding of who He is.

The endeavor to comprehend God and His various attributes should be paramount in our exploration of the Bible. Most of us are inclined to read the Bible with an attitude of "what's in it for me?" Instead, we should consider studying His Word with a desire to see God and His attributes—a God-centered approach.

Man-Centered or God-Centered Theology

When faced with difficulties, we might ask:

"Why is this happening to me?"

"God, don't You care how I feel?"

"What have I done to deserve this?"

"If God really cared, would He allow this?"

Feeling this way, as an initial reaction, is quite normal. However, to ask these questions *after* an evaluation of our situation? This is a denial of God's concern and control. When we relax in His sovereignty, knowing that He knows exactly what He's doing and trusting in His hand, *then* He receives the glory. It is impossible to give God exaltation when we worry or fret.

Is the Creator Incomprehensible to His Creatures?

God cannot be thoroughly understood. A god who is easily and completely known would be a figment of our imagination. Isaiah 55 says, "My thoughts are not your thoughts, neither are your ways My ways. As the heavens are higher than the earth, so are My ways higher than your ways, and My thoughts than your thoughts."

Finite creatures can have only have a limited understanding of an infinite God. He would certainly remain mysterious to us had He not revealed Himself in the unique words of the Bible.

In searching His Word with a desire to see His attributes, you will find your life on a quest filled with golden nuggets scattered along the path—and the excitement of each revelation enabling us to see Him more will highlight this truth more and more. God's mysterious attributes, which are definitely present in the Bible, cannot be understood by lost sinners, and some aspects of His character remain a quandary even to saved sinners. Nevertheless, our admiration and love for His unfathomable traits should not make us anxious. Whether we will ever understand our infinite God is unlikely. Nevertheless, we should treasure what He has revealed about Himself, including His sovereignty in *all things* and *all events*. To those who acknowledge this truth, it is certainly more precious and valuable than anything else.

A New Dimension: Trusting God in Everything

When we are brought, by God's Holy Spirit, to see His sovereignty in everything, and we finally begin to relax in this incredible truth, God is glorified and we are changed. Our outlook is revamped and our insight gains ground as theological questions begin to fit together harmoniously.

One of the overwhelming themes throughout the four gospels is that God wants (and deserves) our trust. He wants us to relax in Him. To give up our desire to be in charge and acknowledge His control—not only in our minds, but our hearts—leading us to a place where we can give Him *all* the glory. This is the exact opposite of pride, and there's no place for pride in our lives.

ABIDING IN HIM

In John 15, Jesus tells us to abide in Him. What does that really mean?

Several Wycliffe Bible translators in South America had a difficult time translating the word "abide" to the tribesmen they were working with. They were invited to go hunting with some of the villagers. When it came time to lay down their spears at the end of the first day and set up camp for the night, they tied their hammocks to trees so they could sleep in comfort and safety from the creatures on the ground.

While they were watching the men suspend their rope-and-mesh beds, the translators suddenly realized the word they had been looking for: "hammock"!

When Jesus describes what we are to do, He says to "abide in Me." In other words, "hammock in Me" or "rest in Me." We are to trust fully, to relax, in our God. For us to shed our prideful concept of control and arrive at the realization that God is sovereign in all things gives us peace and good reason not to worry. It helps us understand why worry is wrong. But the greatest effect it has on our lives is this: our orientation of reliance on God becomes an attitude of praise and glory to Him—in everything that happens.

To relax in the knowledge that everything is under His watching eyes and His controlling hand: what could be more beautiful?

Oprah's Greatest "Aha" Moment

Oprah Winfrey has interviewed thousands of people and had many guests who made her feel like she was seeing something for the first time. Something that would change her life and her entire perspective. Such moments are referred to as her "aha" moments.

One of those guests, on January 4, 1990, helped Oprah see something that she declared to be the greatest aha moment of her career. Her guest explained to her that "Forgiveness is giving up the hope that the past could be any different."

Oprah explained that forgiveness is not just accepting that it's okay that something has happened, but to "give up the hope that things could have been different. Wishing that things would have been different is futile. Don't hold on, wishing that things in our past would have been different."

She explained that this took her to the next level toward being a better person. She now sees the fallacy of holding grudges for anything. Oprah phrased it like this: "Let go of the past so that it does not hold us hostage."

Undoubtedly, she is right.

What's interesting is that she came to the top of the mountain and didn't quite look over. In other words, she acknowledged the attitude we should have when we have a correct perspective of God's sovereignty, yet she did not recognize that God deserves the glory—for the good and the bad things that happen.

As Christians, we can see that the past is not something we should ever regret, no matter how bad it has been. However, going a step further and giving up the hope that things could have been different is actually our opportunity to say, "Praise God. He is sovereign."

What has happened is because God is in control. Not only do I give up on the hope that it could have been different, but I give God the glory because He is in control. So many horrible things happen in this world. This idea of giving God the glory in all things is entirely foreign to most of us. But if we're going to claim that we believe in an omnipotent, omniscient, and sovereign God, then this must be our attitude.

Oprah Winfrey saw the truth about the past and has evidently adopted it into her beliefs. We should all adjust our thinking similarly. Seeing God's hand in this great truth brings Him the glory and honor He deserves.

When Children Die

Explaining God's controlling hand to grieving parents has been a very humbling experience. To have the opportunity to declare God's sovereignty in my child's death or another child's death is still difficult. Yet, there is healing and maturity in this perspective. One mother told me, after the shock of hearing that God had planned her child's death, "You know, I'd rather know that my daughter died as a part of God's sovereign plan than by some accident beyond His control."

As Job said, "The LORD gave, and LORD has taken away; blessed be the name of the LORD" (Job 1:21).

SUMMARY: Most Christians have not truly evaluated this important issue. While most would agree that God is omnipotent—or sovereign— they really have not taken the time to think through all the implications of what that entails. The tendency is to think of God as an "allowing God," not a "controlling God." That is Deism, not Christianity.

Quotes Worth Requoting

"Most Christians salute the sovereignty of God but believe in the sovereignty of man."—R.C. Sproul

"The truths of God's sovereignty are like land mines planted throughout scripture. Not to kill. But they do explode and destroy trivial notions of God Almighty."—John Piper

"Our duty is found in the revealed will of God in the Scriptures. Our trust must be in the sovereign will of God as He works in the ordinary circumstances of our daily lives for our good and His glory."—Jerry Bridges

"God is not an actor within the larger scheme of things. He is not a muscle-bound Jupiter, bullying the little ones. He is the Author of the whole thing. We never ask how much of Hamlet's role was contributed by Hamlet, and how much by Shakespeare. That is not a question that can be answered with 70/30 or 50/50 or 90/10. The right answer is 100/100. Hamlet's actions are all Hamlet's and they are all Shakespeare's."—Douglas Wilson

"There is no greater discovery than seeing God as the author of your destiny."—Ravi Zacharias

"No surer way will be found to fill the mind at one time with reverence, humility, patience, and gratitude than to have it thoroughly saturated with this truth of predestination and God's sovereignty in all things."—Loraine Boettner

"But when God looks at a painful or wicked event through his wide angle lens, He sees the tragedy or the sin in relation to everything leading up to it and everything flowing out from it. He sees it in all the connections and effects that form a pattern or mosaic stretching into eternity. This mosaic in all its parts—good and evil—brings Him delight."—John Piper

"That God predestines, and that man is responsible, are two things that few can see. They are believed to be inconsistent and contradictory; but they are not. It is just the fault of our weak judgment. Two truths cannot be contradictory to each other. If, then, I find taught in one place that everything is fore-ordained, that is true; and if I find in another place that man is responsible for all his actions, that is true; and it is my folly that leads me to imagine that two truths can ever contradict each other."—Charles H. Spurgeon

"If there is one single molecule in this universe running around loose, totally free of God's sovereignty, then we have no guarantee that a single promise of God will ever be fulfilled."—R.C. Sproul

"Everything that exists—including evil—is ordained by an infinitely holy and all-wise God to make the glory of Christ shine more brightly . . . Adam's sin and the fall of the human race with him into sin and misery did not take God off guard and is part of His overarching plan to display the fullness of the glory of Jesus Christ."—John Piper

"That which should distinguish the suffering of believers from unbelievers is the confidence that our suffering is under the control of an all-powerful and all-loving God. Our suffering has meaning and purpose in God's eternal plan, and He brings into our lives only that which is for His glory and our good."—Jerry Bridges

"There is *no middle ground* between the absolute sovereignty of God and total atheism." Charles H. Spurgeon

And finally, Blaise Pascal, in a wonderful letter written to a grieving friend, instead of repeating the ordinary platitudes of consolation, comforted him with this truth:

"If we regard this event, not as an effect of chance, not as a fatal necessity of nature, but as a result inevitable, just, holy, of a decree of His Providence, conceived from all eternity, to be executed in such a year, day, hour, and such a place and manner, *we shall adore in humble silence the impenetrable loftiness of His secrets; we shall venerate the sanctity of His decrees; we shall bless the acts of His providence;* and uniting our will with that of God Himself, we shall wish with Him, in Him and for Him, the thing that He has willed in us and for us for all eternity."

CHAPTER 2

IS GOD SOVEREIGN OVER FREE CREATURES?

Goal & Purpose:
Most Christians today consider themselves to be
autonomous, or in control of their own destiny. Practical
individuals will stubbornly deny God's hand in every detail
of our lives, including their freedom in the decision process.
Yet, God's sovereignty and man's will are parallel truths,
a beautiful paradox. This chapter attempts to reveal in
simple terms a somewhat unnecessarily complex subject.

This chapter and the next are a discussion of two related subjects: God's will and man's "free will." Volumes have been written on these two issues, however, it is my hope that these very important topics can be reviewed here with clarity and brevity.

Many pastors will state that God has two wills: His perfect will and His permissive will. Some also promote the idea that man has a free will, entirely free from any influence or determination by God.

A biblical understanding of these two important subjects is critical, particularly in regards to the development of an accurate theology. As stated earlier, nothing is as important as theological truth, and these two issues—God's will and man's will—are pivotal. Perhaps more than any other area of belief, these issues will influence how we live our daily lives and how we come to understand God.

Some important questions to think about with regards to man's free will:

Is man completely free in his ability to make choices?

Does God have any role in our decisions?

Does God determine the events and situations that influence our decisions?

If so, to what degree?

Is our personal responsibility diminished if God determines our decisions?

Can man's will alter God's will?

What does the Bible say about this?

Helpful Terms and Definitions

Will—The function of choosing.

Constraining causes—Forces that cause people to act against their will, such as a gun pointed at them in a robbery.

Nonconstraining causes—Forces that are sufficient to cause an action, such as the fear of heights, which would likely keep someone off a tall ladder or a roof.

Determinism—The belief that all actions, thoughts, responses, decisions, etc. are causally determined. Every event is the result of other events and conditions.

Indeterminism—The belief that all actions are entirely free and not the result of outside causes.

Incompatibilism—The notion that determinism and free will are incompatible.

Compatibilism—The belief that determinism and free will are compatible.

Libertarian free will—The ability to either do something or not, free of determinism.

Free agency—The ability to do something or not, apart from constraining causes.

(The difference between libertarian free will and free agency is important. Do non-Christians have the inherent ability to choose to trust in Christ or not? Is such a decision ultimately dependent on their own will?)

God's general sovereignty—The belief that God is in charge of everything and able to control everything, but does not.

God's specific sovereignty—The belief that God ordains everything and controls everything to accomplish His purposes and will. (See appendix D for a further exploration of this.)

The Truth Is in the Paradox: Theological and Biblical Reasons for Compatibilism

Our English language is somewhat limited here, but using the term *paradox,* or perhaps *conundrum,* will help to introduce us to compatibilism. Two situations or circumstances are simultaneously taking place. As we explore this a little further, you will see that compatibilism is not difficult to recognize and appreciate. It is an important reality that helps many biblical issues come together that initially appear to be contradictory.

A differing view, however, is libertarian free will, which is traditionally assumed by most in our churches today. This concept has no biblical basis. The Scriptures never tell us that humans are autonomously able to make decisions that are not caused by anything. Free will, in this sense, is often assumed without any evidence from God's Word. On the other hand, Scripture clearly teaches that *God is absolutely sovereign.* He "works all things according to the counsel of His will" (Ephesians 1:11). He does whatever He wants, and no one can stop Him (see appendix A.)

Scripture also tells us that humans are morally responsible, which requires their freedom to make decisions and to be responsible. However, there is no biblical reason that God cannot *cause* human choices, minor decisions and major ones, even as human beings make them. Human accountability finds its biblical basis in God's authority and sovereignty, with Him as our Creator, Sustainer, and Judge—not in libertarian free will.

On the other hand, compatibilism is seen throughout the Bible. Consider the following passages and observe a) God's specific sovereignty and b) human free agency. In every case, *they are simultaneous.*

"The heart of man plans his way, but the LORD establishes his steps . . . The lot is cast into the lap, but its every decision is from the LORD." (Proverbs 16:9, 33)

"This Jesus, delivered up according to the definite plan and foreknowledge of God, you crucified and killed by the hands of lawless men." (Acts 2:23)

"For truly in this city there were gathered together against Your holy servant Jesus, whom You anointed, both Herod and Pontius Pilate, along with the gentiles and the peoples of Israel, to do whatever Your hand and Your plan had predestined to take place." (Acts 4:27-28)

Judas, Joseph's brothers, and Pharaoh all acted with *free agency,* not *libertarian free will.* Judas was destined to betray Jesus. Joseph's brothers acted according to God's purpose and plan as they sought to do away with him. Pharaoh stopped the Jews from leaving Egypt as our sovereign God continually refrained from softening his hardened heart.

The interconnectedness of everything is incredibly complicated. While one small event can influence other events as time goes by, it is remarkably easy to see that God is either in control of everything or nothing at all. Consider this example: what if Adolf Hitler's grandparents, Johann Baptist Poelzl and Johanna Huettler, had not lived in the same village and married? The course of history would have been changed. In fact, your parents or grandparents might not ever have met without the far-reaching influences of World War II.

Since Scripture tells us that God planned your life before creation, then hundreds of people before you had to meet and cross paths—and if any one person in your lineage had taken a different direction or had perhaps the slightest change in their life, you would not be here. (See appendix D.)

If God did not direct every detail of human history, then He could not plan your life. He is in charge of everything or He is in charge of nothing. At the same time, the free agency of human beings plays into God's plans. Compatibilism is seen throughout history, theology, and our daily lives. God used humans to write Scripture. Without violating their volition, He breathed and moved them to compose. The way that God inspired and moved the scribes requires compatibilism.

Our Salvation and Security

A Christian's solid position of safety, known by most of us as eternal security, is the result of God's sovereign hand. God is the one who enables Christians to persevere. In fact a true believer should never fear the loss of salvation. While we may think we have God's hand, He has ours. The absence of determinism, God's controlling the hearts and desires of man, would allow room for Christians to remove themselves from their salvation. Yet we can rest in Paul's words in Romans 8:29, where he states,

> "For whom He foreknew, He also predestined to be conformed to the image of His Son . . . Who shall separate us from the love of Christ? Shall tribulation, or distress, or persecution, or famine, or nakedness, or peril, or sword? . . . For I am persuaded that neither death nor life, nor angels nor principalities, nor powers, nor things present nor things to come, nor height, nor depth, nor any other created thing, shall be able to separate us from the love of God which is in Christ Jesus our Lord."

Paul's list here clearly indicates that nothing can separate the believer from Christ. Not even the misunderstood idea of man's "free will" can separate a true child of God from the Father.

Is Free Will the Key to Being Free?

Will the redeemed be able to sin in Heaven? Since the obvious answer is no, then it is easy to see that we will not have a "free will" in the libertarian sense. *Thus, it is not necessary for us to have a free will to be genuinely free.*

This subject begs the question: did Adam possess free will?

The answer seems to be yes (1 Timothy 2:14, Genesis 3:6).

Is free will the reason Adam and Eve sinned? Eve was clearly deceived by the serpent. We are not clearly told why Adam also ate, but it is apparent that he was free to choose.

Was God surprised when Adam sinned? That answer is a definite no.

Some have adopted the notion that God had to go to "Plan B" after sin entered the human race. This is incorrect. His Word tells us that our lives, and His plan of redemption, came before creation and the fall. *Most theologians hold that God planned the fall, in that it certainly came as no surprise to Him.* After Adam and Eve's sin, did He feel that He had made a mistake in creating man and woman? Definitely not.

Matthew 25:34 describes the kingdom as it was prepared for Christ's redeemed "from the foundation of the world," and Ephesians 1:4 reads, "Just as He chose us in Him before the foundation of the world, that we should be holy and blameless before Him." We also read in 2 Timothy 1:9 of Him "who has saved us, and called us with a holy calling, not according to your works, but according to His own purpose and grace which was granted to us in Christ from all eternity."

OUR FUTURE IS NOT
DEPENDENT UPON FREE WILL—
OUR DESTINY RELIES ON HIS
SOVEREIGN CHOOSING.

If God was surprised at man's first sin, He might have destroyed them right then. However, the fall and the curse were part of God's amazing plan. A plan that is bringing Him glory. *God in no way compelled man to fall.* He merely *withheld* that undeserved constraining grace with which Adam would surely not have fallen—the grace He was under no obligation to bestow. In respect to himself, Adam might have withstood the temptation to sin had he so chosen, but in respect to God's plan, it was certain that he would fall. *He acted as freely as if there had been no decree, and yet as infallibly as if there had been no liberty.*

Free Will and Fulfilled Prophecy

Were the men who carried out the crucifixion of Jesus free to break His legs as they walked in front of the three crosses? They broke the legs of the two thieves! While they were free to break Jesus's legs, it was impossible for them to do so as it was not God's will. We know this for two reasons: First, that's not what happened. *And everything that happens is within God's will.* Second, we are given the prophecy in Psalm 34:20 that not one of Jesus's bones would be broken.

God accomplishes all things according to the counsel of His will, and He ordained that sin would enter His universe through Adam and Eve. He sovereignly works through secondary causes such as humans, weather, earthquakes, etc. <u>God is not culpable of evil—but the secondary causes are</u>. When Pharaoh did not let the Jews leave Egypt, his heart was hardened, which was its natural state in that he was a sinful man (like us all). It was God's sovereign withholding that allowed Pharaoh's heart to remain hardened. Hitler was evil, and he operated with the same sinful propensity that we all have. God obviously withheld His restraint in ways that allowed Hitler to be extremely evil, yet even he did not carry out his evil tendencies to their fullest possible extent. God's restraint was even present in Adolph Hitler.

Satan sinned. Adam and Eve sinned. They are morally responsible to God for it.

The ability to sin has four historical stages:

1) Adam and Eve were initially *able to sin.*
2) After their fall, all their offspring—including us—possess a sin nature. We are *not able not to sin.* It's our nature.
3) Those whom God has brought to Himself, redeemed humans whom He has granted a new spirit, *are able not to sin.*

4) Those who have been granted the gift of repentance and given faith, trusting in Jesus's finished work on the cross, these will be given new bodies after judgment day and will forever *not be able to sin.*

We cannot explain exactly how God can ordain all things without being the author or agent of evil. *However, we cannot deny explicit statements of Scripture that support the idea that we are free agents with responsibilities and decisions, yet God is sovereignly in control of everything, including the choices we make.* We need to acknowledge that this is an enigma that finite and fallen humans simply cannot comprehend exhaustively.

Two Parallel Lines

How can we be responsible for decisions if God is ultimately in control?

A full understanding of our responsibility, or free will, in light of God's sovereignty is difficult—maybe even impossible. However, God never asks us to reconcile these two teachings. The Bible simply teaches both truths. Consider these words from Charles Spurgeon on this issue:

"These two truths, I do not believe, can ever be welded into one upon any human anvil, but one they shall be in eternity: they are two lines that are so nearly parallel, that the mind that shall pursue them farthest, will never discover that they converge; but they do converge, and they will meet somewhere in eternity, close to the throne of God, where all truth does come and go."

J.I. Packer sees these two issues, our responsibility and God's sovereignty in all things, as an *antinomy* rather than a paradox. He explains that we should put down any semblance of contradiction to the deficiency of our own understanding. We should not think of these two principles as rivals, but as complementary to each other. (See graphic in appendix C.)

There is a balance in what we do versus what God does. However, we should understand that it is by God's will that we do our part. He is the one who created us, sustains us, and gives us the mind and will to think and do what we do. He places us in the situations we're in (good or bad) and gives us the gifts of wisdom and trust.

Proverbs 3:5 reveals this balance well: "Trust in the LORD with all your heart, and lean not on your own understanding; in all your ways acknowledge Him, and He shall direct your paths." Knowing that He gives us this attitude of trust, we are to take the action of trusting God with all our hearts! We are to give up trying to lean on our own understanding as to how He guides us. Like the great hymn by John Sammis suggests, "Trust and Obey."

From Your Head to Your Heart

As God reveals His sovereignty to you, this amazing truth will completely change your thinking. Every aspect of a Christian's outlook is transformed when he or she comes to a deeper understanding of God's amazing plan that includes every leaf that falls, every cancer cell that develops or dies, the finest details of a sunset, and the precision of a deadly tornado that destroys a home.

Laying hold of this truth in your mind is important. It is vitally basic to a proper understanding of the Scriptures. When this awareness gets deep into your heart, your life will forever change. The result is a heart of trust, and *nothing is sweeter to our Savior than the trust of those He has redeemed.* When we relax in His mighty hand and His sovereign plan, He is glorified!

John Piper offers this perspective as to why God ordained the origin of sin:

"The ultimate answer . . . Is that "all things were created through Christ and for Christ," Colossians 1:16. God foresaw all that Satan would do if He created Satan and permitted him to rebel. In choosing to create him, He was choosing to fold all of that evil into His purpose for creation. *That purpose for creation was the glory of His Son. All things, including Satan and all his followers, were created with this in view."*

When "Free" Men and Women Are Saved

Perhaps it is in the mystery of conversion that man's will and God's sovereignty are most clearly seen. We know that conversion consists of turning from sin toward God, which is repentance and faith. (Like two wings on an airplane, both repentance and faith are equally emphasized in the New Testament.) But why would a lost sinner turn to God—or turn away from his sin? Is it because of his libertarian free will? Or is it ultimately because of God?

Nonbelievers will not (they cannot) want to make Christ their master unless God changes their desires. Scripture is exhaustive in declaring man's enmity and aversion to God. In fact, natural man is "dead in his sins" (Colossians 2:13, Ephesians 2:1). Lost men are not struggling and drowning, hoping for a lifesaver. Lost men are dead at the bottom of the ocean.

Jesus tells us clearly in John 15:16, "You did not choose Me, but I chose you, and appointed you that you should go and bear fruit." And in John 6:44, "No one can come to Me unless the Father who sent Me brings him." So our freedom is real, yet it hinges on God's sovereign plan and inception. When we initially think that we have chosen Christ, we should realize that He chose us. He's the one who opens our eyes and changes our hearts. Starting out we may think it's our autonomy or personal wisdom that has brought us to trust in Jesus. However, a Christian's growth in the Bible should make him see that it was really God's doing.

SUMMARY: It's a mystery that when Jesus came to earth, He was (and is) 100 percent God and 100 percent man. Likewise, it is a mystery that we have a responsibility to make decisions while God is simultaneously in control of each choice.

We must realize both are true. God has a role in bringing evil about, and in doing so He is holy and blameless. God does bring sinful individuals into position to do what they do, but always for His own good purposes. So in bringing sin to pass, He does not Himself commit sin.

Our finite minds cannot fully understand this quandary. However, we can trust that both aspects of human choice and God's sovereignty are true.

Interestingly and amazingly, they both lead us to glorify God. To deny or diminish all the aspects and particulars of these truths is a denial of God's amazing sovereignty and plan for man.

Quotes Worth Requoting

"We are not saved against our will—but God changes our will." —Ralph Erskine

"Free will I have often heard of, but I have never seen it. I have always met with 'will', and plenty of it, but it has either been led captive by sin or held in the blessed bonds of grace."—Charles H. Spurgeon

"Man is nothing, he has a free will to go to Hell, but none to go to Heaven. Until God works in him—to will and to do His good pleasure."—In a letter from George Whitefield to John Wesley

"There has been no such thing as freedom since Adam fell. Adam was free. Not a single child of Adam has ever been free . . . Man's will has been bound ever since the fall of Adam. By nature man is not free to choose God . . . Do not talk to me about 'free will'; there is no such thing. *There is no such thing as free will in fallen man. The Bible teaches that.*"—Martin Lloyd-Jones

"Free will doctrine. What is it? It magnifies man into God. It declares God's purposes null, since His will can not be carried out unless men are willing. It makes God's will a waiting servant to the will of man."—Charles H. Spurgeon

"Ralph Erskine, in speaking of his own conversion says, *'He ran to Christ with full consent against his will'*—by which he meant *it was against his old will;* against his will as it was until Christ came, but when Christ came, then he came to Christ with full consent, and was as willing to be saved—no, that is a cold word—delighted."—Charles H. Spurgeon

"No power but that which gave life to the world, can give eternal life . . . This new creature is not born of flesh, or of blood, nor of the will of man, but of God."—John Flavel

"The Holy Spirit is no skeptic & the things He has written in our hearts are not doubts or opinions, but assertions—surer & more certain than sense & life itself."—Martin Luther

"Assuming that the serious intentions of God are swayed, and in some cases defeated, and that man, who is not only a creature but a sinful creature, can *exercise veto power over the plans of Almighty God,* is in striking contrast with the Biblical idea of His immeasurable exaltation."—Loraine Boettner

"God saves sinners: *God*—the Triune Jehovah, Father, Son and Spirit; three Persons working together in sovereign wisdom, power and love to achieve the salvation of a chosen people, the Father electing, the Son fulfilling the Father's will by redeeming, the Spirit executing the purpose of Father and Son by renewing. *Saves*—does *everything,* first to last, that is involved in bringing man from death in sin to life in glory: plans, achieves and communicates redemption, calls and keeps, justifies, sanctifies, glorifies. *Sinners*—men as God finds them, guilty, vile, helpless, powerless, unable to lift a finger to do God's will or better their spiritual lot."—J.I. Packer

"Every choice we make is free. Every choice we make is determined."—R.C. Sproul

CHAPTER 3

GOD'S WILL: MAYBE IT'S NONE OF OUR BUSINESS

Goal & Purpose:
Many of us struggle to a degree, some more than others,
to know God's will for our lives. My hope is that you
will see that this does not need to be a confusing matter.
As we increasingly understand God's sovereignty—in
all things—we can relax into an abiding position. There
are standards given to us in Scripture; in applying
those principles and then easing up on the reins, our
relaxation will give Him glory in what He's doing.

The next time you get into your car, suppose that your first three turns are left-hand turns, then a right-hand turn which takes you to a red light. Five seconds later a blue Ford will pull up behind you. Twelve seconds later the light will turn green.

Was every detail of this scenario in God's will?

Was every detail planned by God?

Does God only care about the "big stuff"? Do the little details fall from His concern or control?

Does God have multiple options that He places before us each day, with a new "program" that is set into motion tomorrow as we make choice A, B, or C today?

You have likely heard that God has two or three different wills. This leaves some with the misconception that our Creator might suffer from divine schizophrenia. The other option is that many theologians, pastors, and Sunday school teachers suffer from severe interpretive confusion. The latter is surely the case.

We have been presented with the thought that God has multiple wills associated with a slew of names and descriptions. Several of these have similar meanings, some do not. The following list helps to show the confusion that exists about this important question: *"Does God have more than one will?"*

Several names that have been used to describe God's will:

- Permissive will
- Perfect will
- Effectual will
- Decreed or decretive will
- Sovereign will
- Efficient will
- Secret will
- Revealed will
- Will of command
- Preceptive will
- Perceptive will
- Moral will
- Will of sign
- Will of pleasure

Scripture is quite clear that there is only one "will of God"—no matter how many names and descriptions theologians formulate, God is all-powerful, and all things that occur are within His view and command. Nothing happens beyond His ability to see or change what occurs; therefore, all things that happen before Him are in His control and part of His will. Otherwise, we must assume that God is not omnipotent and omniscient.

In essence, this is what God does by His unlimited power and knowledge: He exerts His sovereign will. He causes what has been ordered and determined to happen from the beginning, all for His glory.

Will the Source of Confusion Please Stand Up?

The confusion about multiple wills can be greatly reduced if we see the contrast between *disposition* and *will*. Understanding the will of God is somewhat confusing because our language does not differentiate between God's decreed will and the will of His disposition. The word *will* seems to have at least two different meanings in Scripture. (This is one reason to honor context when studying the Bible!) Much confusion about this simple misunderstanding has resulted in tremendous rifts and quarrels between believers over the centuries.

When we see that God's will of disposition (His propensity, inclination, proclivity, readiness, or tendency) is different from His decreed will of determination (the events that actually play out), many of the verses that seemed confusing before will suddenly make sense. For example, a simple reading of Scripture will reveal that God seems to have one will that desires *all* to come to repentance and faith. However, Scripture is quite clear that God chooses those to whom He grants the gifts of repentance and faith. It is unquestionable: *not all are saved,* and this seems to contradict His desire or disposition.

In fact, we should know that *God acquires everything He desires.* He's God.

Therefore, it is elementary to see that there must be a secondary meaning to the word *desire* when we are referring to God's will.

Consider the two categories of God's sovereign will.

God's sovereign (decreed) will should be thought of in two distinct ways:

1) What has happened before this moment.
2) What will happen after this moment.

What has happened before this moment always falls within *God's perfect and sovereign will.* Everything that has ever happened, 100 percent of the time, can be considered His sovereign, perfect, and decreed will.

What will happen after this moment can be considered to fall within God's secret will. This too is His decreed and sovereign will, just as *all* the things that have happened in the past.

The reason we use the term "secret will" or "secretive will" is this: *it is not revealed to us—nor is it any of our business*. To try to know God's secret will apart from His revealing it can be considered divination or soothsaying, similar to those who might be seeking to look into a crystal ball, read horoscopes, consult tarot cards, or visit psychics. And these are prohibited practices according to Scripture.

Psalm 25:14 in the King James Version reads, "The secret of the Lord is with them that fear Him; and He will shew them His covenant." God may show us aspects of His will, but it is He who causes, shows, and reveals. It is not our job to somehow "divine" it. In fact it is the fear of the Lord that initiates this revelation, and that fear itself is from Him.

God's "Disposition"—Not His Sovereign Will

Perhaps the strongest passage in the Bible that states God's desire to save all is 1 Timothy 2:3-4: "For this is good and acceptable in the sight of God our Savior, who desires all men to be saved and to come to the knowledge of the truth." A casual reading of this passage seems to indicate that God will have everyone to be saved. We know by observation of the world around us and by Scripture that all are not saved.

So, the possible alternatives are:

a) This biblical teaching is wrong.
b) God's sovereign will is that all be saved, and He is unable to fulfill His own will.
c) "All" does not always mean all.
d) The term "will" means something different than His sovereign will, such as "His disposition."

Anytime we see the word *will* in conjunction with God's desire to save all or to "bring everyone to Himself," it can be interpreted as His disposition. With this understanding, it becomes evident that His will, in terms of His sovereign will which cannot be contravened, and His

29

will in terms of His disposition are different things and not in conflict. Again, it seems that God's disposition is to save all, but His sovereign, perfect will is to save some.

Of course, in this case, we can also see other clues in the context that unlock a fuller understanding of the passage. <u>Does God desire for every person to be saved?</u>

Consider this:

1) Can God miss out or come up short in acquiring what He desires? Of course not. He always gains what He desires. He's omnipotent, omniscient, and sovereign.

2) Could terms like "all" and "everyone" possibly be misunderstood?

In Acts 2:5 and 21:28, we are told that "every Jew from every nation under heaven" was there at Pentecost, and the Jews who were opposed to Paul said he was teaching to everyone, everywhere. There are many examples in the Bible where *every* and *all* are general terms— not absolute or emphatic expressions. It is consequential to understand that *all* in Scripture does not always mean every individual. In fact, it usually means *all kinds of people*—different backgrounds, nationalities, skin colors, ethnicities, social classes, etc. (see Revelation 15:4; Psalm 22:27, 65:2, 66:4, 72:11; Isaiah 66:23.)

Inclusive terms in the Bible, such as *every, everyone, all,* and *the world,* will usually mean *all groups,* especially in the New Testament letters. Keep in mind that the Jews, and most of the early church which was made up of Jews, had a strong tendency to think the gospel and salvation were for the Jewish people only. They had been God's chosen people for centuries, and Jesus, the Messiah, was a Jew.

To get over this tendency, *the writers emphasized that the gospel was for every group.* All the classes and nations. Not exclusively for the Jews. Therefore, *all* was used in this context in many passages throughout the New Testament. Understanding that God is not partial was difficult for many in the early church; consequently, there is a strong emphasis in New Testament writing that shows God saves people *in ALL parts of the world and from EVERY group.* Rich or poor, educated or clueless, no matter where someone is born or to what culture; *God chooses to save people from every corner of the world.*

Let's look at the rest of Paul's paragraph in verses 5, 6, and 7:

"For there is one God and one Mediator between God and men, the Man Christ Jesus, who gave Himself a ransom for all, to be testified in due time, for which I was appointed a preacher and an apostle—I am speaking the truth in Christ and not lying—a teacher of the Gentiles in faith and truth."

Notice his emphasis on the Gentiles. He is making it again clear: the gospel is for "all" peoples, not the Jews only.

In summary, passages like 1 Timothy 2:3-4 can be interpreted two ways: a) inclusive terms like *all* and *everyone* can mean every group or nation, or b) the term *will* means that God has a propensity to do something, yet His ultimate and determined action can be different.

Seeing the Word *Will* in Two Different Ways

1) Will: God's determined plan. Everything that happens.
2) Will: God's disposition. What He is inclined to do. Propensity.

Jonathan Edwards, born in 1703, considered by many to be the greatest thinker and theologian in the past five hundred years, stated:

"When a distinction is made between God's revealed will [disposition] and His secret will, or His will of decree, "will" is certainly in that distinction taken in two senses. His will of decree, is not His will *in the same sense* as His will of command. Therefore, it is no difficulty at all to suppose, that the one may be otherwise [different] than the other: His will in both senses is His *inclination* . . . His will of decree is His inclination to a thing, not as to that thing absolutely, but with respect to the universality of things.

Though He hates sin in itself, yet He may will to permit it, for the greater promotion of holiness in this universality, including *all things, and at all times.* So, though He has no inclination to a creature's misery, considered absolutely, yet He may will it, for the greater promotion of happiness in this universality."

When God's inclination to lavish His creation is interrupted with sin, then that lavishing does not happen. Even though *He could stop sin,* He has chosen to allow it for a time—and He clearly tells us that it is for His ultimate purposes and glory. *This is a mystery we finite sinners cannot fully comprehend regarding our infinite Creator and Sustainer.*

Two Analogies

Two correlating stories may be helpful in conveying the difference between God's disposition and His sovereign will. The first one involves something that happened to me last year.

Our family had a pit bull that was reluctantly allowed to live on our twenty acres. The dog seemed very gentle and got along with the other animals, even the cats. One day I was on the tractor and saw dust flying and a commotion. Realizing that this dog had grabbed one of our miniature donkeys by the jaw and was pulling it to the ground, I ran to the donkey's aid. Yelling at the pit bull was useless as he pulled the much larger animal to the ground. I kicked the dog with my boots several times. Even kicking him in the throat was of no effect. My brother-in-law quickly brought me a rifle. Two rifle shots finally stopped the jaws that were relentlessly holding the injured miniature donkey on the ground. The dog was dead, yet it would have never occurred to me that morning that I would be killing an animal, much less one of my own, by the end of the day. *In this case, my disposition and my actions were different.*

My nature or propensity is to take care of animals. However, the introduction of the evil nature of that dog caused me to do something outside of my normal propensity. This analogy is like most analogies that we use to describe God—very limited and somewhat incongruous. However, for some it may help convey the idea of God's sovereign will of decree in contrast to His revealed disposition.

The second analogy is an account from the life of George Washington that John Piper cites from the writings of Robert Dabney and Chief Justice Marshall's book, *Life of Washington*. "A certain Major Andre had jeopardized the safety of the young nation through 'rash and unfortunate' treasonous acts," Marshall says of Major Andre. The young major was very popular and admired by many, including George Washington. After Andre's arrest, Washington signed the order in the fall of 1780 to have him executed. It was entirely *against* Washington's inclination or propensity to have Major Andre hanged. Dabney recorded that General Washington's compassion was "real and profound."

Washington held the "power to kill or to save." Why did he sign the death warrant? Robert Dabney explains, "Washington's volition to sign the death-warrant of Andre did not arise from the fact that his compassion was slight or feigned, but from the fact that it was rationally counterpoised by a complex of superior judgments . . . of wisdom, duty, patriotism, and moral indignation."

These stories illustrate the fact that a will of disposition and what actually happens can be, and usually are, divergent. We are aiming to better understand how these two "wills" work together in harmony.

D.A. Carson holds to this same understanding:

"We cannot do without some distinctions concerning the "will(s)" of God. Both in the Old Testament and in the fourth Gospel, not to say elsewhere, God is sometimes presented as the one who seeks men out, loves a lost world, declares his yearning for their repentance, and the like. *This "will" of God is his disposition; it is not necessarily his decree. But precisely how both operate in one sovereign God is extremely difficult to understand.*"

The Reformed Dutch theologian Herman Bavinck gives the following excellent summary of the matter:

"Over and over in history we see the will of God assert itself in two ways.

1) God commands Abraham to sacrifice his son, yet He does not let it happen (Genesis 22).

2) He wants Pharaoh to let his people Israel go, yet hardens his heart so that he does not do it (Exodus 4:21).

3) He has the prophet tell Hezekiah that he will die; still He adds fifteen years to his life. (Isaiah 38:1 & 5).

4) God prohibits us from condemning the innocent, yet Jesus is delivered up according to His definite plan and foreknowledge. (Acts 2:23; 3:18; 4:28).

God does not will sin; He is far from iniquity. He forbids it and punishes it severely, *yet it exists and is subject to His rule* (Exodus 4:21; Joshua 11:20; I Sam. 2:25; 2 Sam. 16:10; Acts 2:23; 4:28; Rom. 1:24, 26; 2 Thessalonians 2:11; etc.). *He desires the salvation of all* (Ezekiel 18:23, 32; 33:11; I Tim. 2:4; 2 Pet. 3:9), *yet has mercy on whom He wills and hardens who He wills.* (Romans 9:18)."

Bavinck continues,

"Just as a father forbids a child to use a sharp knife, though He Himself uses it without any ill results, so *God forbids us rational creatures to commit the sin that He Himself can and does use* as a means of glorifying His name. *Hence, God's hidden will and His revealed will are not really incompatible,* as the usual objection has it. For in the first place, God's revealed, perceptive will is not really His ultimate, sovereign will but only the command He issues as the ruler for our conduct. In His perceptive will He does not say what He will do; it is not the rule for His conduct; *it does not prescribe what God must do, but tells us what we must do.* It is the rule for our conduct (Deut. 29:29). *It is only in a metaphorical sense, therefore, that it is called the will of God.*"

Am I in God's Will? How Do I Know?

Attending a Baptist church in Texas when I was young left me with the idea that I needed to focus on staying in God's will. Knowing whether I was in God's will or not was a silent mystery. But it sure seemed like there must be two or more wills for God. So how was I supposed to know how to "stay" in God's will?

As the years went by, it seemed like there were times when I could say, "Yes, that's God's will," and other times I knew (or so I thought) that I was definitely *not* in God's will. Still, my premise was unsound and certainly not based on good biblical training.

The best answer I've heard to the question, "How do I know if I'm in God's will?", is this: "Look around. You're right in the middle of it."

What if you're attending a school that you're not sure about, or married to someone who makes you doubt your judgment? Suppose you're working in a factory and wondering why you didn't study harder in school? Or perhaps you're sitting in jail. *The fact is, wherever you are, you're smack-dab in the middle of God's will.*

If God had two or three alternative pathways that could somehow lead us to where we are to go, then we would certainly have a reason to wonder if we are in His will, but that's not the case. Consider too, the interconnectedness of virtually everything that happens. (Appendix E)

What Should Our Attitude Be Toward God's Will?

Should we attempt to follow our heart or focus on renewing our mind by digging into His Word? Our concern with respect to God's will and the future is summed up in Romans 12:1 and 2:

"I beseech you therefore, brethren, by the mercies of God, that you present your bodies a living sacrifice, holy, acceptable to God, which is your reasonable service. And do not be conformed to this world [age], *but be transformed by the renewing of* your mind, *that you may prove what is that* good and acceptable and perfect will of God."

Our responsibility is to focus our minds on the Word of God. The common misconception that many Christians have adopted from the world of "following your heart" is antithetical to the Bible. In fact, Scripture is very clear that our hearts are scheming and untrustworthy (consider Jeremiah 17:9 and Genesis 8:21). But a heart saturated in God's Word, with a propensity that matches biblical principles, is another matter. The first three verses of the book of Psalms demonstrate this clearly. Keep in mind that the heart is a metaphor that represents the deepest aspects of our mind:

> "Blessed is the man
> who *does not walk in the counsel of the wicked*
> or stand in the way of sinners
> or sit in the seat of mockers.
> *But his delight is in the law of the Lord,*
> *and on His law he meditates day and night.*
> He is like a tree planted by streams of water,
> which yields its fruit in season
> and whose leaf does not wither.
> Whatever he does, prospers."

The term "his delight is in the law of the Lord" means to delight in the instruction and the words of the Lord. This is very simple, but true. If you desire to know and do God's will in your life and with your decisions, your highest priority should be "renewing your mind," and that is done through reading and studying God's Word. That kind of renewing and transformation can occur only as the Holy Spirit changes our thinking through consistent study and meditation on Scripture.

Again, that is the major reason for this book. We need to dig into God's Word with the intention of finding areas in our theology that might be off base, with a willingness to get a tune-up. *The Bible is a living tool of communication from God to each of us.* Hebrews 4:12 tells us, "For the word of God is living and active and sharper than any two-edged sword . . . Able to judge the thoughts and intentions of the heart." Matthew 4:3-4 says, "It is written, 'Man shall not live on bread alone, but on every word that proceeds out of the mouth of God.'"

Steps to consider when seeking direction:

A) *Read your Bible.* Paganism says to "empty your mind"—the Bible says to "fill your mind."
B) *Think biblically.* This comes from reading and studying God's Word.
C) *Pray biblically.* Know that prayer is "articulated trust"—pray scripturally and use Scripture to pray.
D) *Seek wise counsel.* From others who are wise and biblically minded.
E) *Repeat.*

Thwarting the Influences of This World

As we seek to renew our minds according to the Word of God, Paul warns us "not to be conformed to this world [or age]." Many today have allowed Christianity to be compromised by several major areas of influence. Some churches even associate themselves with various aspects of the following:

1) *Education:* The average child attends school for fourteen thousand hours. The public schools as a whole have a mandate to be anti-Christian.
2) *Media:* Much of the mindless entertainment we celebrate is opposed to biblical principles and oftentimes has us hoping for the bad guys. Marriage is taboo, and sex out of marriage is presented as the norm.
3) *Psychotherapy and psychology:* These are antithetical to the Bible. The Bible teaches that our greatest problem is inside of us, with our sin nature, and the solution is God's Word and His guidance by His Holy Spirit. Most psychologists teach the opposite— that our problems are outside of us and our solutions are from within.
4) *Liberal theology:* This is the concept that it doesn't really matter what you believe, yet you can still ascribe to some of the more

popular teachings of Jesus, such as how we treat the poor or "do unto others as we would have them do unto us." Most would not teach the inerrancy or sufficiency of Scripture and would certainly not endorse a literal understanding of Genesis or the sovereignty of God. Today, most of the universities that were founded on sound, biblical principles have become centers of advancement for liberal theology.

SUMMARY: It is invaluable to understand that the word *will* in Scripture is oftentimes a description of God's disposition or inclination. This is helpful in our understanding that *God has one will:* His perfect, decreed will.

When seeking God's will, or direction, in our lives, we should avoid the world's opinions and fill our minds with His Word, seeking advice from other like-minded believers as well.

Quotes Worth Requoting

"It implies no contradiction to suppose that an act may be an *evil act, and yet that it is a good thing that such an act should come to pass* . . . As for instance, it might be an evil thing to crucify Christ, but yet it was a good thing that the crucifying of Christ came to pass."—Jonathan Edwards

"It is a profound political reality that Christ now occupies the supreme seat of cosmic authority. The kings of this world and all *secular governments may ignore this reality, but they cannot undo it.* The universe is no democracy. It is a monarchy. God himself has appointed his beloved Son as the pre-eminent King. Jesus does not rule by referendum, but by divine right. In the future every knee will bow before him, either willingly or unwillingly."—R.C. Sproul

"At the end of that time I, Nebuchadnezzar, looked up toward Heaven. My mind became clear again. Then I praised the Most High God. I gave honor and glory to the One who lives forever.

His rule will last forever.
His kingdom will never end.
He considers all of the nations on earth
to be nothing.
He does as he pleases
with the powers of heaven.
He does what He wants
with the nations of the earth.
No one can hold His hand back.
No one can say to Him,
'What have You done?'"
—Daniel 4:34-35

"The larger our enterprise is, the more important it is that we shall have *a plan;* otherwise all our work ends in failure. One would be considered foolish who undertook to build a ship, or a railroad, or to govern a nation without a plan. We are told that before Napoleon began the invasion of Russia he had a plan worked out in detail, showing what line of march each division of his army was to follow, where it was to be at a certain time, what equipment and provisions it was to have, etc.—Whatever was wanting in that plan was due to the limitation of human power and wisdom. Had Napoleon's foresight been perfect and his control of events absolute, his plan—or we may say, his foreordination—would have extended to every act of every soldier who made that march."—Lorraine Boettner [Loraine Boettner, 1901 to 1990, is considered one of the great modern writers who could describe theological issues clearly. His favorite song was, understandably, "A Boy Named Sue."]

CHAPTER 4

DECISIONAL REGENERATION: DOES THE BIBLE TEACH SALVATION BY DECISION?

Goal & Purpose:
Many think that salvation is the result of making a decision. The
Bible is clear that those who are chosen by God for salvation
are brought to Him by His own hand. He grants the gifts of
repentance and faith *and* the "decisions" that are made. These are
the result of God's mercy. This chapter is intended to help clarify
the beautiful and amazing truth that God plans, achieves, and
completes our redemption. Hopefully this will help reveal the myth
of salvation by decision which is prevalent in our churches today.

"You did not choose Me, but I chose you."—John 15:16

*"So then, it does not depend on the man who wills or the man
who runs, but on God who has mercy."*—Romans 9:18

Altar calls.
Decisions for Christ.
Sinner's prayers.
Asking Jesus into your heart.
To reduce salvation to a mere decision is demeaning to the entire
plan of redemption and to the life and death of Christ. In many churches,
asking people to make a "decision for Christ" and perhaps come forward
during an "altar call" can be well intentioned, but it is terribly out of
line with the New Testament. In fact, this is a recent phenomenon that
finds its roots in the mid-1800s.

With good intentions, many preachers and evangelists use techniques developed to mass-market the gospel. This approach is foreign to anything seen in the early church or the lives and ministries of the apostles. These methods are also theologically foreign to their writings.

Encouraging a "Decision for Christ": What Is Implied?

When preachers encourage their listeners to "make a decision for Christ," several things are implied.

1) Your decision saves you.
2) This is something that *you* have done.
3) You have been convinced or have seen enough evidence. Now you should make this decision.
4) Jesus's work on the cross is insufficient, since you still have to do your part to complete the process.
5) Since it's your decision that has brought you salvation, you can change your mind later.
6) It was your decision, your wisdom, your ability to make this choice that has saved you.
7) Insistence on decisional regeneration does not reflect a humble heart. It implies that your salvation was a cooperative effort: God did His part and you did your part.

Most pastors will instruct their congregations that they can be assured of their salvation because they have "made a decision" to follow Christ. While it is true that Christians can be very assured of their future with Christ in Heaven, that assurance should not be implied to be the result of a decision.

In churches or at evangelistic crusades, this "decision" is often a collaboration of several things that make its significance seem even more viable. For example, a decision with a walk forward to the altar and a prayer (usually known as "the sinner's prayer"). These three acts—along with a sincere heart—are all you need to be saved. At least that's the illusion.

Emotions and music often play a major role in bringing results. There are several hymns that have been used for decades, sometimes being played over and over, to compel those in the service to walk down the aisle or raise their hand. The raising-hands method usually involves the preacher saying, "with heads bowed and eyes closed." I once heard a music leader at a megachurch talking about how the band could predict which chords or parts of the "invitational" songs would produce the most response.

A Common Analogy— And the Truth It Betrays

For years, evangelists have used a common analogy at the end of their sermons to prompt a decision by unsaved individuals in the congregation. It goes like this:

"Imagine you fell overboard from a ship and you were struggling in the icy waters to stay afloat. Bobbing up and down, fighting to keep your head above the water, hoping that someone on board would throw you a life ring and rope. Suddenly, you see out of the corner of your eye the white ring floating just a few feet away. All you need to do is reach over and grab ahold—you'll be safe."

The piano is playing softly, and then the speaker tells everyone, "The life ring is right here—right now. Grab ahold and come forward. Let us pray with you. Don't leave this place today without making this important decision. Come now."

This analogy is gripping, moving—and wrong. It betrays a basic theological problem at the root of "decision-based" salvation. The problem with the analogy is this: the lost are not floundering on top of the water looking for a life ring. They're dead at the bottom of the ocean.

God saves people dead in their sins. He takes them off the sea floor and breathes new life into them. *Dead people don't decide to be saved.* God does it all.

"And you were dead in your trespasses and sins." (Ephesians 2:1)

"For as the Father raises the dead and gives them life, so also the Son gives life to whom He will." (John 5:21)

"Even when we were dead in our trespasses, He made us alive together with Christ—by grace you have been saved." (Ephesians 2:5)

"And you, who were dead in your trespasses and the uncircumcision of your flesh, God made alive together with him, having forgiven us all our trespasses." (Colossians 2:13)

Before today's emphasis on decision-making and "praying the prayer," baptismal regeneration was a common false teaching. This heterodoxy was succeeded by decisional regeneration (there are still vestiges and occasional signs that some still believe in salvation by water baptism).

In the early 1800s Albert G. Finney, considered by most church historians to have been a heretic, brought man-made techniques into the pulpit. He taught that the teaching and preaching of the gospel should be presented in ways that produced visible response and results. He said, "A revival is as naturally a result of the use of means as a crop is of its appropriate means." His use of the term "means" can be taken to mean techniques, procedures, performance, tactics, routines, strategy, etc.

The idea of persuading or motivating people to come forward to the "anxious bench" or "altar" as it is referred to now (a glaring misuse of the term) developed during this time. Finney popularized salesmanship and brought closing techniques into the pulpits of America. He admitted that truth and theology were boring to him. Although many pastors did not agree with his methodology, his ideas have managed to creep into mainstream churches over the past century.

False Conversion and True Conversion

These tactics were effective in bringing numbers of people to the front of churches at the end of sermons—however, most, if not virtually all, have proven to be false conversions. Sadly, altar calls, especially the emotionally charged ones, bring people forward who are then told that the "decision" they're making is salvation.

The vast majority of the people who go forward for these "invitations" never stay around for more than a few weeks. Some estimates put the number at 90 percent. The disgraceful thing about this is that these people have been told, for the most part, that their decision to come forward and "accept Jesus" and pray with the pastor or counselor has assured them of eternal life in Heaven.

None of us know what's in a man or woman's heart—but to counsel them with a message that tells them they are saved because they made a decision is wrong.

Some pastors justify this sort of ministry with the hope that getting people to make a commitment—whether they're genuinely saved or not—will at least provide them with an opportunity to experience some good discipleship training. The problem is that discipleship can not take the place of true conversion. Discipleship of goats is not conversion, and it certainly does not produce sheep. Bad teaching that produces false converts, with a little discipling then added to the mix, does not take the place of authentic salvation.

True conversion is entirely different. Salvation is easy in that it is the work of God and we can't earn our way to Heaven. It is Jesus's finished work on the cross. Period.

The repentance and faith that we have to trust in Jesus's amazing act of obedience unto death—for our salvation—is from God. That is salvation!

When that trust in Jesus is genuine, it will change your life. Your desires and direction change. You begin to love what God loves and hate what God hates. God hates sin, so you begin to despise any sin in your life. (Note that this is self-directed—it's not an intrusive or nosy attitude focused on the lives of others and their wrongdoings.) You experience a relentless desire to please God and live a life motivated with a thankful heart. A thankful heart motivates you because of what has already been done for you; it is not an attempt to please God in order to gain His favor.

And what is the purpose of salvation? To produce acceptable worshipers of our amazing Creator, Savior, and Sustainer.

Does God Fish with an Enticing Lure—Or a Net?

The two most common ways fish are caught:

1) By appealing to or wooing them with a lure
    or
2) By capturing them with a net.

We've all tried to catch fish with bait or a lure. As a sport fisherman myself, and having attended several fishing seminars sponsored by lure manufacturers, I've heard it said many times: "It's all about the presentation."

Preachers today who are working in the tradition of Albert G. Finney must think their job is to have a great-looking lure and know how to work it so it will bring in the most fish. While attending church in my teen years, I heard a pastor explain John 6:44, which says, "No one can come to Me unless the Father, who sent Me, draws him." The preacher explained that the term "draw" means "wooing" or "enticing."

That is incorrect.

The word "draw," as it is used here, is the same Greek word, *helkuo*, which is used in John 21:6: "They cast therefore, and now they were not able to draw it, for the multitude of fish." They were pulling in fish, or drawing them in, with a net. None of those fish were "wooed" or "enticed."

When a net is cast—fish don't have any choice.

When God draws—He gets what he casts for.

Jesus made it very clear in John 15:16: "You did not choose Me, but I chose you."

This is further emphasized in Ephesians 1:3-4:

"Blessed be the God and Father of our Lord Jesus Christ, who has blessed us in Christ with every spiritual blessing in the heavenly places even as He chose us in Him before the foundation of the world."

If He chose us before creation—which He clearly has done—then our salvation was His choice. He knows exactly where the net is going, and He's always successful with His casting and His drawing in. Nor does God's casting have anything to do with the quality of the fish, so to speak. We don't earn our salvation: we simply receive it.

Abraham and Israel—Simply Chosen

Were Abraham or any of his lineage, the Jewish nation, worthy of God's attention? What made them any different from the other kingdoms or nations in Abraham's day? Nothing.

This is another major facet of biblical salvation. God chose Israel for His own reasons, not because they deserved anything special (see Isaiah 45:4, Amos 3:2, and Deuteronomy 7:7 and 9:4-6). Likewise, He chooses individuals for salvation apart from any merit of their own (see Matthew 24:24 and 24:31, Romans 8:29-33, Ephesians 1:3-6, Colossians 3:12, Titus 1:1, and 1 Peter 1:2.)

Some may find this doctrine troubling, asking, "But what if He didn't choose me?" Those who are preoccupied with this subject are most likely to be among those He is drawing into His net. It seems extremely unlikely that anyone with a genuine interest in this question is among those who are not being drawn and saved.

Think about it. So few people are really interested in the truth of God's Word. Even fewer are concerned to learn more about His attributes and His ways of redeeming the lost. It's hard to imagine that anyone would see the truth presented in the Scripture, have a desire to be among the chosen, and *not* be in the net already. Not all fish perceive their capture—initially.

If someone truly wants to be among the chosen, then it's obvious they probably are. If they have genuinely repented of their sin (turned 180 degrees from their former desires and sins) and placed their faith and trust in Jesus's finished work on the cross, then they *are* chosen. Only those whom God chooses have been granted the gifts of repentance and faith.

Jesus said, "All that the Father gives Me will come to Me, and whoever comes to Me I will never cast out" (John 6:37). Those whom the Father has chosen will come to Him. If you have a desire to be His, that desire came from Him!

So, To Be Saved, Do I Make a Decision or Not?

In regards to God, you do make decisions. In fact, you probably made several decisions along the way to your salvation. You decided to agree with God's Word that you are guilty of sin. You decided to be concerned that you would be guilty on judgment day. You decided to place your trust in Christ.

It's also accurate to say that this was the most important decision of your life. However, it's not the decision that saved you.

Consider this twofold explanation:

First, the decisions you make are from God. He is the one who gives you desire for Him and softens your hard heart. You can be stubborn and declare that your decisions are your own. However, that doesn't seem to be reflective of a contrite heart, broken over sin and thankful to your sovereign Creator for bringing you to Himself.

Second, it's not your decision that saves you. It's God's mercy and amazing grace that saves you.

There are decisions involved in your salvation! The key is that the decisions don't ultimately come from you. It's difficult for some headstrong people to concede: however, God is sovereign and He gives you everything needed to make those decisions.

This really is quite profound.

Sure, it's your decision to repent and put your faith in Christ. But it's only because of your omnipotent and merciful God that you make decisions—good and bad. This particular decision cannot be made by anyone unless God first draws him. Therefore, He receives 100 percent of the glory.

Is Jesus Standing at the Door Knocking?

No. He's not.

The image of Jesus standing at the door, knocking, waiting to be let in so that we can be saved, is commonly used in evangelistic appeals. It's similar to the life ring—we just need to make a decision to open the door. But the idea that our Creator is waiting for us is an inaccurate and misguided concept that has saturated the church today.

This notion puts us in the driver's seat and places God in a position of waiting on us. Biblically, this is terribly inaccurate. Can you see Jesus standing at the door, waiting and wishing Johnny or Sally would just open the door to let Him in?

This image comes from a passage in Revelation 3. It is addressed to the angel of the church in Laodicea. Verse 20 reads, "Behold, I stand at the door and knock. If anyone hears My voice and opens the door, I will come in to him and eat with him, and he with Me."

The passage is clearly not addressed to the world, but to the church in Laodicea, and it makes clear that the way of repentance and hope is open to those whom God draws. The common usage of this passage is out of context. Even so, it does offer a message of hope. Despite the disgusting and offensive conduct of the Laodiceans, Jesus has forgiveness even for those within that group who repent and trust in God's mercy.

If We Hold to the Idea of Decisional Regeneration . . .

Most Christians who hold to the teachings surrounding decisional regeneration believe that Christ died for the sins of every person in the world, and it's now up to each individual to accept this gift. Should the message of Jesus's salvation inspire or cause them to finalize the process by deciding to follow Him or pray for forgiveness, then the steps of salvation have been completed. However, if they reject this message and God's gift of mercy and grace, they have decided on their own to go the opposite direction.

A.W. Pink summarizes this notion well. He states in his classic book, *The Sovereignty of God,* this important point:

> "To say that God the Father has purposed the salvation of *all* mankind, that God the Son died with the express intention of saving the *whole* human race, and that God the Holy Spirit is now seeking to win *the world* to Christ; when, as a matter of common observation, *it is apparent that the great majority of our fellow men are dying in sin,* and passing into a hopeless eternity;
>
> This is to say that God the Father is *disappointed,*
>
> That God the Son is *dissatisfied,*
>
> And that God the Holy Spirit is *defeated.*
>
> There is no escaping the conclusion. *To argue that God is "trying His best" to save all mankind,* but that the majority of men will not *let Him* save them, is to insist that *the will of the Creator is impotent,* and that *the will of the creature is omnipotent.*
>
> To throw the blame, as many do, upon the Devil, does not remove the difficulty, *for if Satan is defeating the purpose of God, then, Satan is Almighty and God is no longer the Supreme Being."*

Caution: Sloppy Language

If you spend time around any of the larger Protestant churches or the new megachurches dotting the evangelical horizon, you'll hear statements like this:

"We had three decisions for Christ last Sunday."

"The youth meeting Friday night had two decisions and four recommitments."

Or someone might ask:

"When did you accept Christ?"

(By the way, who are we to "accept" the God of the universe? We don't accept Him—He's the one in the position to do the accepting.)

To demean the miracle of redemption to a term like *decision* gives it the nuance of a business opportunity before us, like Amway or some multilevel marketing proposal. As ambassadors of Christ we have a responsibility to use accurate language. Words are important, and some words carry an inaccurate connotation.

Consider what it would be like hearing comments like these:

"Last Wednesday night three young people were brought to Christ by His amazing mercy."

"Last week God softened Ralph's heart, gave him the gift of repentance, and granted him the faith he needed to put his trust in Jesus for the forgiveness of all his sins."

"This morning one of the teens visiting our church declared that she had turned from sin and is now trusting in Jesus for her forgiveness."

Wow!

You might think, "That's sure a lot of words. Wouldn't it be easier to stick with something easier and shorter?"

Yes. But what can be more important, and what should be more accurate, than our words? Especially the words describing someone's eternal salvation! Nothing could be more important.

Conversion and the Role of Emotions

Do emotions play a legitimate role in coming to Christ?

Sure they do. We all have emotions, and they are vitally important and critical in many of our decisions. Career choices, sports we play or watch, whom we marry—these are undoubtedly surrounded by emotions. But they are not necessarily *based* on intuition or feelings. And here is the critical distinction.

When God brings us to the realization that He is a holy God and that we are guilty sinners unable to spend eternity in His presence without the removal of our sins, we should develop some deep emotions! When He shows us what His Son did on the cross, the love and kindness of that act should create an intense and extraordinary feeling of thankfulness and relief.

However, the emotional circus that is created by certain church leaders in order to push people to make a decision or "come forward while the Spirit is leading" is nothing more than manipulation.

A Final Challenge

As you seek to be more biblical in your thinking, consider taking these words or terms out of your vocabulary when it comes to how you refer to salvation: "decision," "accept," and "ask Jesus into your heart." These are certainly not biblical, nor do they give honor to God for the absolutely incredible and extraordinary way He saves us.

James Adams, the author of a great booklet entitled *Decisional Regeneration,* ends with this summary and challenge:

"It is not a time to be silent; it is time to speak out. We have kept quiet too long, somehow feeling that if we opposed these unbiblical practices we might be hindering the good work of evangelism, hoping that among the multitudes of "decisions" there are some genuine conversions. But, with every passing week, thousands are being counseled into a false hope! Sinners are directed to walk down aisles and to make decisions, when they should be pointed to Christ alone. The high calling of preaching has degenerated into a series of gimmicks and tricks. These false practices have resulted from the perversion of Biblical doctrine. Therefore, in the midst of this darkness, let us pray that God may be pleased to revive His Church again. This revival can only come through Christ. Men must turn afresh to Christ's directions for counseling, for the preaching of His Gospel, and for calling sinners to repentance and faith. Only then will our labors bring glory to God; and if God grants, many sinners will be converted for His glory."

SUMMARY: Are we saved by making a decision? No. Does God use decisions along the path of our salvation? Yes. We need to acknowledge that God is the one who saves us. He doesn't just buy the ticket—He takes us all the way there. When we see this more clearly, it helps our understanding of His sovereignty *in all things* and makes it instinctive for us to give Him glory with our thinking and the words we use.

The following Scriptures teach us the truth about our salvation. May we be faithful to accurately convey the truth and bring God glory, remembering He is the one who saves us and He is the one who sustains us. We are not saved by a decision, nor can we become unsaved by a decision.

"Not everyone who says to Me, "Lord, Lord," will enter the kingdom of Heaven, but only he who does the will of My Father who is in Heaven." (Matthew 7:21)

"All things have been committed to Me by My Father. No one knows the Son except the Father, and no one knows the Father except the Son and those to *whom the Son chooses* to reveal Him." (Matthew 11:27)

"But, to all who did receive Him, who believed in His name, He gave the right to become children of God, who were *born, not of blood nor of the will of the flesh* nor of the will of man, but of God." (John 1:12-13)

"For as the Father raises the dead and gives them life, so also the Son *gives life to whom He will.*" (John 5:21)

"All that the Father gives Me will come to Me, and whoever comes to Me I will never cast out." (John 6:37)

"No one can come to Me unless *the Father who sent Me draws him.*" (John 6:44a)

"My sheep hear My voice, and I know them, and they follow Me. I give them eternal life, and they will never perish, and no one will snatch them out of My hand. *My Father, who has given them to Me,* is greater than all, and no one is able to snatch them out of the Father's hand." (John 10:27-29)

"You did not choose Me, but *I chose you* and appointed you that you should go and bear fruit." (John 15:16a)

"When they heard these things they fell silent. And they glorified God, saying, 'Then to the Gentiles also *God has granted* repentance that leads to life.'" (Acts 11:18)

"The Lord opened her heart to pay attention to what was said by Paul." (Acts 16:14b)

"For the mind that is set on *the flesh is hostile to God,* for it does not submit to God's law; indeed, it cannot." (Romans 8:7. A rebellious sinner cannot choose to follow God. God must do the changing first.)

"For those whom *He foreknew He also predestined* to be conformed to the image of His Son, in order that He might be the firstborn among many brothers." (Romans 8:29)

"And those whom *He predestined He also called,* and those whom He called He also justified, and those whom He justified He also glorified." (Romans 8:30)

"Who shall bring any charge against God's elect? It is God who justifies." (Romans 8:33)

"So then it *depends not on human will* or exertion, but on God, who has mercy." (Romans 9:16)

"So then He has mercy on whomever He wills, and He hardens whomever He wills." (Romans 9:18)

> Not only does God choose who will be saved,
> but this obviously means that He chooses
> who will *not* receive His mercy.

"But who are you, O man, to answer back to God? Will what is molded say to its molder, 'Why have you made me like this?' Has the potter no right over the clay, to make out of the same lump one vessel for honorable use and another for dishonorable use? What if God, desiring to show His wrath and to make known His power, has endured with much patience vessels of wrath prepared for destruction, in order to make known the riches of His glory for vessels of mercy, which He has prepared beforehand for glory— even us whom He has called, not from the Jews only but also from the Gentiles?" (Romans 9:20-24)

"The natural person *does not accept* the things of the Spirit of God, for they are folly to him." (1 Corinthians 2:14a)

"For He chose us in Him before the creation of the world to be holy and blameless in His sight. *In love He predestined* us to be adopted as His sons through Jesus Christ, in accordance with His pleasure and will—to the praise of His glorious grace, which He has freely given us in the One He loves." (Ephesians 1:4-6)

"In Him *we were also chosen,* having been predestined according to the plan of Him who works out everything in conformity with the purpose of His will." (Ephesians 1:11)

"And you were *dead* in the trespasses and sins." (Ephesians 2:1)

"For it is by grace you have been saved, through faith—and this not from yourselves, it is the gift of God—not by works, so that no one can boast." (Ephesians 2:8-9)

> Some think that believing in God's
> sovereignty in salvation means that there's
> little or no need to spread the gospel.
> This verse, among many others,
> makes it clear that God chooses—
> yet the gospel still needs to be presented.

"But, we ought always to thank God for you, brothers loved by the Lord, because from the beginning *God chose you* to be saved through the sanctifying work of the Spirit and through belief in the truth. *He called you to this through our gospel,* that you might share in the glory of our Lord Jesus Christ." (2 Thessalonians 2:13-14)

"Those who oppose him, he must gently instruct, in the hope that God will *grant them repentance* leading them to a knowledge of the truth." (2 Timothy 2:25)

"Peter, an apostle of Jesus Christ, *to God's elect,* strangers in the world, scattered throughout Pontus, Galatia, Cappadocia, Asia and Bithynia, who *have been chosen* according to the foreknowledge of God the Father, through the sanctifying work of the Spirit, for obedience to Jesus Christ and sprinkling by His blood: Grace and peace be yours in abundance." (1 Peter 1:1-2)

"Who according to His great mercy has *caused* us to be born again to a living hope through the resurrection of Jesus Christ from the dead." (1 Peter 1:3)

Quotes Worth Requoting

"As we had nothing to do with our physical birth, but received it as a sovereign gift of God, we likewise have nothing to do with our spiritual birth but receive it also as a sovereign gift."—Lorraine Boettner

"If the final decision for the salvation of fallen sinners were left in the hands of fallen sinners, we would despair all hope that anyone would be saved."—R.C. Sproul

"It is necessary, therefore, to take the thought of human responsibility very seriously indeed. But we must not let it drive the thought of divine sovereignty out of our minds. While we must always remember that it is our responsibility to proclaim salvation, we must never forget that it is God who saves."—J.I. Packer

"A man is not saved because he believes in Christ; he believes in Christ because he is saved."—Lorraine Boettner

"We talk about predestination because the Bible talks about predestination. If we desire to build our theology on the Bible, we run head on into this concept. We soon discover that John Calvin did not invent it."—R.C. Sproul

"In modern day evangelism, this precious doctrine of regeneration has been reduced to nothing more than a human decision. To raise one's hand, walk an aisle, or pray a 'sinners prayer.' As a result, the majority of Americans believe that they've been 'born again' even though their thoughts, words, and deeds are a continual contradiction to the nature and will of God."—Paul Washer

"As a human being I might prefer that God give his mercy to everyone equally, but I may not demand it. If God is not pleased to dispense his saving mercy to all men, then I must submit to his holy and righteous decision. *God is never, never, never obligated to be merciful to sinners.* That is the point we must stress if we are to grasp the full measure of God's grace."—R.C. Sproul

CHAPTER 5

DOES PRAYER CHANGE THINGS?

Goal & Purpose:
Prayer is not a tool or method for us to plead with
God. It should not be a means by which we attempt
to change God's mind toward what we want.
Prayer should be evidence of our reliance on Him
as our sovereign Creator and Sustainer.
Our prayers do not change God's plan.
Prayer is to align our hearts with His plan
and acknowledge our trust in Him.

Traditionalism has put forth the idea that events are changed by our fervent prayers. The belief that "if we pray" the future might be different is common to most branches of the church today.

How many times have you heard, "Prayer changes things?" What does that really mean or imply?

Does it mean that the sovereign and perfect will of God is diverted or fine-tuned when we pray?

When we pray, are we hoping that an illness or some circumstance facing a loved one will be changed whether or not our request is in accord with God's will?

What does it mean to pray in Jesus's name? Is that the "abracadabra" that makes our prayers heard, or is it equivalent to saying, "Whatever is Your will?"

Since we know, through God's Word, that He has a predetermined plan for the events in our lives (see appendix A), is it our hope that our prayers might change these events? Or should our prayers be for the purpose of bringing our needs to God with the intention of *showing our reliance on Him?* Should we have a desire to develop hearts that are in tune with His plan, whatever it brings?

> "Prayer is not overcoming God's reluctance.
> It is laying hold of His willingness."
> —Martin Luther

As we seek to bring our understanding of prayer in line with what the Bible really teaches, we could add that it should not be our hope that things will be different than His mighty plan, but that we would see and trust in His sovereign will despite what our flesh may want. We seek an attitude of dependency on God and a desire to have our hearts in tune with His purposes.

Articulated Trust

It can be said that prayer is articulated trust. This is not a trust that God will grant all our requests, like a genie in a bottle, but a reliance on God's will—whatever it may be. Even though we do not always include this in our words, it should be clearly understood, when we pray, that His will is the dominant factor and interest.

Those reading this might say, "Well then, if God has a perfect plan and His will is unchangeable, why should I pray? It's useless to pray." This attitude then becomes the basis of defeatism. Caution!

The popular song "Que Sera, Sera (Whatever Will Be, Will Be)" was the theme music for *The Doris Day Show* from 1968 to 1973. It qualifies as the anthem of fatalism or defeatism, which is an apathetic attitude of resignation. *It is not a Christian attitude.*

Contentment and trusting in God's powerful and precise hand in everything are entirely different from "Que sera, sera." The most striking difference is the heart and a clear understanding that the things that are going to happen come by the hand of the One who created us. We can and should experience a contentment, or even excitement, in knowing that He has designed everything and every event for His purposes.

God's children trusting in His precise supervision is entirely unlike fatalism. A look at the way Jesus taught His followers to pray and the way most of us pray is quite revealing.

"The Lord's Prayer," recorded in Matthew 6:9-13, is the ideal prayer Jesus gave His disciples:

"Our Father in Heaven, hallowed be Your name.
Your kingdom come, Your will be done,
on Earth as it is in Heaven.
Give us this day our daily bread,
and forgive us our debts, as we also have forgiven our debtors.
And lead us not into temptation, but deliver us from evil."

Interestingly, Jesus's ideal prayer for us begins by acknowledging and addressing God as our Father and *hallowing* His name. John Piper tells a story of when he was at the end of a long and exhausting jog and feared he was about to have a heart attack. A prayer came to him which has stuck with him all his life: "Father, don't let me live another day if I'm not an instrument of hallowing Your name." What a great attitude and prayer for any of God's children to wake up to every day!

In the Lord's Prayer, immediately after the introductory emphasis on hallowing God's name comes the clear acknowledgment of God's will. This is not a request that His will will be done—that is certainly the case—*but an acknowledgment of that fact.* Your will be done, on this planet, just as it is in Heaven. When it comes to God's will, there's no difference between Heaven and Earth. It is always achieved in both places.

What About Making Our Requests Known Before the Lord?

So why should we pray to make our requests known when God knows our needs before we even know them?

Why pray when we know His will is perfect and that what is planned will not be changed by our prayers?

Here are a few reasons:

1) We are told to pray and to lay out our needs and concerns in Ephesians 6:18, Matthew 26:41, and Philippians 1:4, as well as in many other passages in God's Word. We pray in obedience to God's clear instruction.

2) When we bring our requests to our Father, it is our acknowledgment of His care for us, trusting that He is watching and listening.

3) Prayer reveals areas of need and brings clarity within our hearts.

4) Prayer is proof of our faith in God. If we had no trust in His listening ear—His concern for our concerns—then we would have no reason to petition Him.

5) Corporate prayer allows us to make needs known before both God and a concerned group of fellow believers. Prayer with others is worship.

Praying for our requests is *not,* as some false teachers propose (usually on television), something that works on a "name it and claim it" principle. This impression of prayer, as taught by many of the "Word of Faith" groups and others, including mainstream denominations, is false and lacks any real biblical basis.

The Effective, Fervent Prayer of a Righteous Man Avails Much

James 5:16-18 tells us that Elijah prayed for a drought for three and a half years, and it did not rain. Elijah, a man no different from us, then prayed for rain—and it rained. As we look at similar Scriptures that tell us about prayers that preceded various events, are we to interpret them to mean that these things happened *because* someone prayed? Or should we see that God's people were given desires or special insight so they would pray for events that were in keeping with God's plan?

While Elijah was a man with a nature like ours (verse 17), he was also a prophet. Those who would be considered "righteous" and are praying fervently would perhaps be blessed with a special ability to pray specifically for an unusual event—such as a forty-two-month drought and the rain that would break it.

All of our prayers should be laid before God with the understanding that we are to desire His will. Certainly Elijah would have prayed the same way. As a result, the fervent prayers of a righteous man truly can be said to avail much: they simply step into the will of God.

However, the Bible also demonstrates that the fervent prayers of a righteous man will not *always* succeed. A righteous man may fervently pray something that is not in accord with the unchanging will of God. Moses and Samuel stood before God, and He said no. Those destined to die by the sword would die by the sword, those destined to die by famine would die by famine, and those destined for captivity would be captured (Jeremiah 15:1-2, Numbers 14:11-25, 1 Samuel 12:19).

In a New Testament example, the apostle Paul was not granted a fervent request. After seeing Heaven, he was in danger of becoming "puffed up" by his extraordinary experience. He was given a thorn in the flesh, as described in 2 Corinthians 12:7-8. However, *Paul certainly did not want it.* He went to the Lord three times asking that it be removed. The thorn was not removed, but God gave him the strength to live with it.

Heads Bowed and Eyes Closed, and Other Magic Formulas

Prayer can be anywhere, anytime. It is a reflection of our trust in God and His purposes at all times, in all things. Therefore, it certainly does not require that we stop and close our eyes. While corporate or group prayer is typically conducted with our eyes closed, this is only to lessen distraction and aid the focus of our hearts and minds in a group setting. It is certainly not a requisite of prayer.

One of the common misconceptions that traditionalism carries is the idea that ending prayers with "in Jesus's name" or "in the name of Christ" is some sort of formula that will legitimize the petition. The heart is the real issue, not our word formula. To apply to God for anything in the name of Christ, our request must be in keeping with who Christ is! To ask God in the name of Christ *is as though Christ were the one asking.*

To ask in the name of Christ, or in Jesus's name, is to set aside our own wills, accepting God's will whatever it may be.

Our Prayers Are Within God's Hand

As we contemplate prayer and God's amazing control in *all* that occurs, it's humbling to realize that our prayers undoubtedly fit within that plan. Just as He has placed your eyes on these words at this moment, *He has given you the heart and mind to pray every prayer you will ever pray.* A stubborn heart will deny this. To affirm, especially after seeing the clear declaration of His sovereignty in all things, that our prayers are a gift from Him—this is to give Him credit for His might and His wisdom. What could be more humbling? What a privilege to be instruments for His glory!

SUMMARY: The way that we understand God affects the way we pray.

Traditionalism's view is that prayer is meant to coax God to fulfill our wish list, no matter how noble it might be. Such thoughts on prayer are due to an inaccurate view of God's attributes, in particular His sovereignty. The Bible teaches that prayer is to hallow God's name with our trust in His will as we express our needs.

If we think of God as benevolent only toward those He's pleased with, or toward those who pray the hardest, then we are praying to a false god—a god we have imagined or created to suit our own ideas. This is a clear violation of the second commandment, which tells us not to create an image of God—whether physical or in our imaginations!

Nowhere in God's written revelation about Himself does He indicate that our requests are contingent upon something we do or believe, such as prayer combined with a garnered-up batch of faith. We are also not to think of prayer as a means of changing God's plan. *He does not have two plans—one based on me praying and one based on my lack of prayer.*

As seen earlier, God's will is perfect. Most importantly, it is something we can relax in—and that relaxation brings Him glory. We should desire to abide in Him, which is to abide in His perfect and sovereign will (John 15:1-17)

Christians should also see that there are two workers at hand in their walk, or more properly understood, their sanctification. We have a decisive worker, who is God. And we have a dependent worker, ourselves. Our task is to declare our dependence on Him all day long. In the apostles' first letter to the Thessalonians, their final instructions included this: "Rejoice always, pray continually, give thanks in all circumstances; for this is God's will for you in Christ Jesus." *That conscious dependence* is the kind of prayer the apostles were likely talking about when they instructed us to pray without ceasing (1 Thessalonians 5:17, Romans 1:9).

In the apostles' first letter to the Thessalonians, their final instructions included this: "Rejoice always, pray continually, give thanks in all circumstances; for this is God's will for you in Christ Jesus."

Quotes Worth Requoting

"Yes, prayer changes things. God ordains what will happen and He ordains the means (our prayers), to accomplish what He has sovereignly planned. It does not change God's will, but it does change things—*in that God uses our ordained prayers.*"—A.W. Pink

"The popular view of prayer reduces God to a servant, our servant: doing our bidding, performing our pleasure, granting our desires." —A.W. Pink

"To say that human destinies may be changed and moulded by the will of man is rank infidelity—that is the only proper term for it. To say that human destiny may be changed by the will of man is to make the creature's will supreme, and that is, virtually, to dethrone God."—A.W. Pink

"Prayer is not overcoming God's reluctance. It is laying hold of His willingness."—Martin Luther

"To affirm that God will not, and cannot bring to pass, His eternal purpose unless we pray, is utterly erroneous, for the same God who has decreed the end has also decreed that His end shall be reached through His appointed means, and one of these is prayer."—A.W. Pink

"The Lord kills and He makes alive: He brings down to the grave and brings up from the grave. The Lord makes poor, and He makes rich: He brings low and lifts up. He raises up the poor out of the dust, and lifts up the beggar from the dunghill, to set them among princes, and to make them inherit the throne of glory."—1 Samuel 2:6-8

"It is not surprising that prayer malfunctions when we try to make it a domestic intercom to call upstairs for more comforts in the den."—John Piper

"If a believer prays in faith and asks for those things which are according to God's will, he will most certainly obtain that for which he has asked . . . God will become more real to him and His promises more precious . . . A prayerless life means a life lived out of communion with God and all that is involved by this."—A.W. Pink

"God does according to His will in the army of Heaven and among the inhabitants of the earth. No one can restrain His hand or say to Him, 'What have you done?'"—Daniel 4:35

"God knows the end from the beginning. To affirm that God changes His plan is either to impugn His goodness or to deny His eternal wisdom."—A.W. Pink

"The key to praying with power is to become the kind of persons who do not use God for our ends but are utterly devoted to being used for His ends."—John Piper

"Ephesians 1:11 expressly declares that God 'works all things after the counsel of His own will,' therefore, it follows that, 'God's policy is not being shaped by man's prayers. Rather, He uses our prayers, which too, work after the counsel of His will.'"—A.W. Pink

"In our requests, we declare His rulership over the whole world." —A.W. Pink

"Prayer is an act of worship. It is the prostrating of the soul before Him; It is a calling upon His great and holy name. It is the recognition of His sovereignty."—A.W. Pink

"Prayer brings glory to God. Nothing from us is so honoring and pleasing to Him as the confidence of our hearts."—A.W. Pink

"Prayer is designed by God for our humbling . . . A sense of His majesty produces a realization of our nothingness and unworthiness." —A.W. Pink

"Prayer is not for the purpose of informing God, as if He were ignorant, it is designed as a humbling confession to Him of our sense of need."—A.W. Pink

"God has decreed the means as well as the end, and among the means is prayer. Even the prayers of His people are included in His eternal decrees. *Prayers have a place in the predestined order of events."*—Robert Haldane

"It is God's purpose that His will shall be brought about by His own appointed means, and those means certainly include prayer."—A.W. Pink

"Jesus knew for certain that after His death and resurrection He would be exalted by the Father. Yet we find Him asking for this very thing: 'Now, Father, glorify Me together with Yourself, with the glory which I had with You before the world was.' Jesus also knew that none of His chosen could perish, *yet He prayed,* 'Holy Father, keep them in Your name, the name which You have given Me, that they may be one, even as We are.'"—A.W. Pink

"No prayer is pleasing to God unless the spirit producing it is: 'Not my will, but thine be done.'"—A.W. Pink

"Even though God's goodness, purpose, and blessings are promised to His chosen—it is our privilege to ask."—A.W. Pink

"Prayer is a coming to God, telling Him my need (or the need of others), committing my way unto the Lord, and then leaving Him to deal with the situation."—A.W. Pink

"Is it said that the promises of God are all-inclusive, and that we may ASK GOD FOR WHAT WE WILL. If so, we must call attention to the fact that it is necessary to compare scripture with scripture to learn the full mind of God on any subject. As this is done, we discover *God has qualified the promises* given to praying souls by saying, 'If we ask anything *according to His will*, He hears us.' 1 John 5:14."—A.W. Pink

"You ask and do not receive, because you ask with wrong motives."—James 4:3

"Do not be anxious about anything, but in everything by prayer and supplication with thanksgiving let your requests be made known to God. And the peace of God, which surpasses all understanding, will guard your hearts and your minds in Christ Jesus."—Philippians 4:6-7

CHAPTER 6

RETHINKING WORSHIP: THE THREE E's

Goal & Purpose:
This chapter addresses the reality that
most "worship" services today are
man-centered rather than God-centered.
The focus in this chapter is worship; in
particular—corporate worship.
An example of a "new" form of corporate
worship is revealed, hoping that pastors
will consider implementing this in their own churches.

What is worship?

The Anglo-Saxon word *weorthscipe,* translated in modern English as *worth-ship,* means: "to give honor and respect."

Webster's Dictionary provides this definition of *worship:* "Giving honor. Holding in high esteem."

For Christians, the simple answer should be: "To give honor and high esteem to God."

For many years, the three E's, *evangelism, education,* and *edification,* have been considered to be worship or a part of worship. Churches meet primarily to pursue these three. However, we should consider a review. Are these really worship?

If we consider *evangelism* to be the focus of any church meeting, then our congregation time doesn't really qualify or meet the clear definition of worship—giving honor and esteem to God. Evangelism is focusing on the lost.

If we consider *education,* even though it may be from God's Word, to be the central goal, then our Sunday morning isn't worship. Education is in fact a focus on ourselves.

Edification, which is the building up or development of one another, is not eligible to be considered worship—it too is focused on ourselves.

This is the important question before us today: is our purpose in corporate worship to make us better and smarter Christians, or to focus our hearts and minds on God and God alone?

This is not a fine line. There is a profound and distinct difference. Is the focus on me? Perhaps on how I can serve the Lord better? On how I can grow spiritually? Could it be that we consider it worship when we make an effort to improve ourselves as Christians?

As noble or well-intentioned as this may seem, such a focus is not congregational worship. If we define worship as *giving* honor to God, is it really fair to say that *acquiring* a series of instructions on the Christian life or even some deep theological issue really qualifies as corporate worship?

Taking time to listen to a sermon—is that worship? Some might argue that it is; that listening to a sermon and participating in a traditional church service is worship. The question is worthy of our careful evaluation. Even though our purpose in an education—or edification-based church service is to become a stronger believer or a better Christian parent or a more spiritually focused person, these things in reality *are me-centered.*

Jesus Himself spoke to us about worship. John 4:23:

"But the hour is coming, and now is, when the true worshipers will worship the Father in spirit and truth; for the *Father is seeking* such to worship Him. God is Spirit, and those who worship Him must worship in spirit and truth."

What an awesome thought. To be among those whom the Creator of the universe, God almighty, seeks to have among His worshipers! This is a privilege we need to appreciate. In fact, this is such an important and astonishing thought that it is worth repeating. *This is an honor we should stop to contemplate: the One who made every planet and galaxy we've seen images of from the Hubble Telescope and the intricate details we see through an electron microscope, that same Creator seeks our worship!*

Jesus tells us, too, that His Father is spirit. Man could never comprehend the invisible God unless He chose to reveal Himself. We see His amazing handiwork, but we cannot see Him. He has exhibited Himself through His creation, His Son and His written Word, the Bible.

On this passage, John MacArthur explains, "The word 'spirit' does not refer to the Holy Spirit but to the human spirit. Jesus' point here is that a person must worship not simply by external conformity to religious rituals and places (outwardly) but inwardly ('in spirit') with the proper heart attitude."

The other important word Jesus uses here is "truth."

Our worship and understanding of God need to be entirely consistent with His revealed words. Knowing the facts about our Father and the truth from His Word is crucial for proper worship. Otherwise, we are attempting to worship a god of our own design in a self-styled manner.

Since truth is such an integral part of worship, it is obvious that we need to be diligent in our study of His Word. But does this mean that studying the Bible in a corporate setting is worship? There's probably not a yes or no answer. But this question is also worthy of reflection.

Corporate Worship and Personal Worship

Like-minded believers who want to share and express their thankfulness to God for who He is and for what He's done: this is the makeup of corporate worship and the only thing needed for it. How those believers choose to express themselves will vary by culture and background. The only real criteria is that they follow biblical patterns and admonitions.

Of course, worship is not limited to gathering with others in a certain place at a set time. Any time we honor our God—individually or assembled with others—we are worshiping Him. When we trust in His sovereignty with a biblically accurate understanding of His attributes and nature, that is worship, in spirit and truth.

Paul tells us in Romans 12:12 to "be constant in prayer," and again in 1 Thessalonians 5:16 to "rejoice always, pray without ceasing."

If we think of prayer incorrectly, then this seems impossible. Even a monk living in a monastery can't be in continuous prayer. Likewise, our perception of worship can be based on a great misunderstanding.

So what is worship?

Personal worship is the result of an attitude of honoring God for His hand in all we see and experience, every waking hour of the day. It is understanding, believing, and treasuring this truth—that He is in control of everything. *This generates an attitude or frame of mind that results in continuous worship.*

Of course, the great limitation here is the fact that we are still sinners (saved sinners!) living in a world of sin with our own physical limitations and struggles. However, when we pause to contemplate who God is, and remember His watchful and controlling hand, we can once again give Him the glory. This is personal worship.

Giving God glory and thanks in all things, trusting Him in all circumstances, includes cancer, car wrecks, drownings, tsunamis, and murder. When we pause and realize that He is in control of all these things too, we can rest in His mighty hand. *Knowing that His purposes are sure*, despite our lack of understanding of why He takes us through turmoil and troubles, *is worship*. When we get our bearings straight and realize who He is, we can worship Him in the hardships. In fact, that's the place from which the greatest praise and worship comes.

Modern Corporate Worship

So how does our typical expression of worship stack up?

The most common scenario today: the service normally begins with a few songs, then a welcome announcement from one of the church leaders, then a prayer and maybe another song (sometimes a hymn with a piano playing, or one of the newer "praise songs" and a praise band). Perhaps then some announcements followed by a thirty-minute sermon. Most sermons are designed to nurture or encourage the members in some way. They usually contain a degree of entertainment and humor, coupled with some Bible verses. Overall, the sermon is a mixture of Bible, current events, and motivational seminar. The primary aim is to inspire and educate the congregation. This is fine—but it's *not worship.*

Just because we call it worship, that does not make it worship?

SEEKER SENSITIVE WORSHIP

When we design our worship services around the lost, we turn the focus away from God and place the accent on those whom we hope to bring into our church.

The reason this issue is important, as we consider true worship, is that the local church has for many years sought to accommodate the lost, or the "seekers." While evangelism is extremely important—and for us a definite privilege and a directive from Jesus—in many local churches, worship time has been compromised to make the lost feel comfortable.

In this, we have weakened or relinquished worship.

In our efforts to attract outsiders, essentially trying to "sell our church"—hoping that it will increase in size—a God-centered approach has become strange and foreign. Church growth should not be the goal; *it should be a byproduct* of our commitment to honor God when we meet.

Should we be seeker sensitive? Should the local church be concerned about the way nonmembers feel when they visit?

Yes. We should be extremely interested in those who visit. They should be treated with genuine hospitality. *But compromising our worship in order to make others comfortable is a mistake.*

Focus on God—Not Ourselves

Before we take a look at something that is beginning to happen in churches around the world, the following analogy may be helpful in our understanding of the importance of focusing our corporate worship time on our amazing Savior and the effect this might have on each of our lives.

Suppose it's early June, and you have a twenty-acre field to mow. As you drive your John Deere to the edge of your field for the first time this year, you think, "It sure would be good to get these lines a little straighter than last year."

So, how do you mow a straight line across a long field?

Well, if you've never tried this, you can even do it in your own backyard. You pick out a tree or fence post—an object at the other end of the field—and you focus your eyes on that point. If you do that—and keep your eyes on the chosen object—you will be pleasantly surprised when you get to the other side. When you turn to look back, the line will be straight.

In true worship, our focus and interest are on Christ. If we corporately, as a local church body, come together once a week to renew our focus on and admiration of Jesus's life and death on the cross, it will do amazing things to our hearts. And when we get to the other side, we can look back—to a much straighter line than we would have imagined possible.

What's really interesting about this comparison is this: _the straight line is not the emphasis, the straight line is the result or byproduct_. As Christians, we should keep our eyes focused on the cross, which is the culmination and center of our faith. If we keep our attention and passion on seeing that, we will find that in the future we can look back knowing that the path we've left behind will be straight.

Consider This Form of Worship . . .

Some churches don't confuse sermons with worship. This is good, because listening to a preacher and weekly announcements is not really worship. Sermons and Bible studies are important. Very important! However, rarely are they a time when the center of attention is devoted to honoring God.

However, another trend is beginning to emerge. Churches adopting it have set aside a designated time of worship. And incredibly, this does not include a sermon. The Bible teaching or sermon comes before or after the worship time, which is usually thirty minutes to an hour long.

This worship period is characterized by several things:

1) There is no leader or pastor.
2) Comments are made by those attending (usually less than five minutes each).
3) Scriptures are read as those attending feel led.
4) Prayers of thanks are made.
5) Hymns and psalms are requested and sung by the congregation.
6) Hymns and psalms are sometimes simply read.

> "What, then, does this mean, brothers?
> *When you gather, everyone* has a psalm,
> teaching, revelation, foreign language, or interpretation.
> Everything must be done for building up."
> —1 Corinthians 14:26

The various comments and the readings are usually focused on the life and death of Jesus as well as God's sovereignty.

Sometimes there are times of silence. Once in a while, gentle weeping is heard. During this worship hour, the elements of the Lord's Table are meditated upon and distributed, sometimes early in the hour, sometimes in the middle or later portion.

This special meeting can be appropriately described several ways:

- "The Worship Hour"
- "The Lord's Table Hour"
- "A Memorial Feast"
- "Covenant Renewal Hour"

This last title seems to suggest a renewing of our commitment, but it is exactly the opposite. The term "Covenant Renewal Hour" indicates in reality a celebration and expression of thankfulness for the constant covenant renewal that God makes with His children. His covenant or contract with us is one-sided. We come with nothing, He comes with everything. He includes us in His wealth. Since the wealth we've inherited comes through the finished work of His Son on the cross, the Lord's Table and a Covenant Renewal Celebration are one and the same.

Order—But Freedom

This form of worship is structured to a degree, but it certainly allows an appropriate measure of freedom. The structure involves a set start and finish time—usually thirty minutes to an hour. It also includes the taking of the elements, the cup and the bread. Requested songs, Scripture readings, comments, and prayers follow a theme during this Christ-centered occasion. Participants try to self-regulate their time to five or six minutes at the most.

Some additional thoughts regarding this form of worship:

1) Like the analogy of mowing a straight line across a field, this focus on the cross helps us to keep our eyes and feet pointed in the right direction the other 167 hours of our week. "Let us fix our eyes on Jesus, the author and perfecter of our faith, who for the joy set before Him endured the cross, scorning its shame!" (Hebrews 12:2).

2) Unlike a typical modern church service where the preacher does 90 percent of the speaking, this format invites individuals to be prepared before they enter, as the Holy Spirit may have a brief message or Scripture reading for them to share with the congregation. (This is not a time for church members to get on their soapbox about some current issue—it should be limited to reverent expressions surrounding God's character and Jesus's death on the cross.)

   During the week, prior to the next meeting, members should be sensitive—or have their antennas up, so to speak—constantly making themselves aware that the Holy Spirit may have something for them to see or observe. What God shows them during the week may be appropriate to share during the next Lord's Table meeting.

3) It is genuinely honoring to God. (Visitors will appreciate that, provided they are seeking a church that has set its priority on honoring God and not programs.)

4) This form of gathered worship seems to be in line with at least two specific aspects detailed in the New Testament:

a) Hebrews 12:28 entreats us to worship with "reverence and awe."

b) First Corinthians 10:16 and Acts 2:42-46 and 20:7 provides us with clear evidence that the early Christians observed a weekly breaking of bread together. This was likely a time that gave honor and reverence to the death of Jesus on the cross. (This breaking of bread may very likely have been a full meal. More and more churches are beginning to implement this as well.)

The Three E's—Yes!

So what about the three E's—evangelism, edification, and education?

They definitely have their place in the church. In fact, *they're of major importance.* They even have a peripheral role in worship. However, they should not be the *center* of our worship. Honoring God should be the highlight and main feature of our time together. It's hard to imagine that we can do both at the same time. That's why a focused time of *worship,* not of preaching or outreach, should be considered by every Christian church.

WHAT IF SEEKERS WERE EXPOSED TO GOD-CENTERED WORSHIP?

Most churches have lost sight of worship in order to supposedly create a comfortable atmosphere for the lost. I use the term "supposedly" because true worship is not offensive. To be in the presence of people who are genuinely, with reverence and awe, worshiping God and focusing their time together on Jesus's life and death on the cross—wow! It seems that would be captivating and interesting to anyone looking for a true encounter with the living God.

To be in the midst of a congregation that is devoted to singing and talking about such an amazing thing as our God and His work of salvation is an incredible experience. It is also such a rarity that many Christians have never actually had this experience themselves! So many churches have missed out on true worship because of the willingness to compromise or design their services and programs around attracting the neighborhood. Interestingly, they would probably "attract" more in their sphere of influence if they were focused on true, God-centered worship.

As we gather to worship, our focus should be on our God—specifically His sovereignty and the accomplishment of Jesus's finished work on the cross. Personally, I find that gathering with like-minded believers once a week to look closely at what God has done through the life, death, and resurrection of His Son is like a farmer keeping his eye on a fence post a quarter mile away. This focal point, the cross of Jesus, becomes the means that enables a straighter line in the footprints I leave behind.

The early church experienced growth because they were excited about the risen Savior. Their excitement and amazement over what God had done in sending His Son was contagious. *His life, death, and resurrection were the focus. Growth was not the goal—it was a natural result.*

Not Enough Time?: A Challenge to Church Leaders

Most churches that have incorporated a participatory worship time consider it to be the main reason they gather, rather than a secondary addition to their schedule. In fact, if you had to restrict your weekly gathering to one hour a week, this would (or should) be the number-one choice. It's certainly the most biblical.

Fortunately, we have more time than one hour to meet.

Some churches have shortened their Sunday school and teaching service in order to provide for a third meeting. One church in Dallas has their Lord's Table Hour in the evening on Sunday. However, most keep it on Sunday mornings.

Here is one way to incorporate a worship hour into a church that has a traditional Sunday morning lineup: eliminate adult Sunday school and rely on home Bible studies to fill that area of fellowship and teaching. This allows for a Bible teaching or sermon time and a one-hour worship time on Sunday morning.

As those who are reading this discover or develop times and places of this form of worship, they are invited to post their information at www.SoWhyDidntTheyTellMeThatInChurch.com. We will devote an area on the site to listing participatory worship times in various geographic areas as we are notified.

Seekers, Worship, and Evangelism

When visiting a church that is having a service without a pastor in the pulpit, where individuals in the congregation get up to briefly speak or read Scripture and the congregation sings reverentially as members make requests—most newcomers are probably somewhat surprised. Maybe shocked.

Perhaps seeing a group of believers honoring God with a genuine, respectful attitude of love expressed in such a unique manner would cause the average seeker to say, "This is different." If they don't like it, that's fine, but if they are truly being drawn by God, it's hard to imagine that they would not want to be present every week.

SUMMARY: In Genesis 1, each day ends with God's declaration, "It is good." At the end of the week, we are told that He rested. There's reason to believe that this "rested" means God admired His handiwork. We know He did not need to rest like we do; however, His declaration that it was good seems to indicate that He paused to admire His creation. Perhaps we should think of worshiping as a pause to admire Him.

Instead of seeing our Sunday mornings as a time to educate ourselves or reach out to our communities, we should instead think of our "day of rest" as a "day of admiration." Affirming together that God is good. We might endeavor to honor Him rather than making education, evangelism, and edification out to be the worship that He seeks. There is plenty of time for these other things.

In this, we declare that we are not the center of our theology—God is.

Quotes Worth Requoting

"What does God want out of a believer? He wants acceptable, spiritual worship."—John MacArthur

"The worship to which we are called in our renewed state is far too important to be left to personal preferences, to whims, or to marketing strategies. It is the pleasing of God that is at the heart of worship. Therefore, our worship must be informed at every point by the Word of God as we seek God's own instructions for worship that is pleasing to Him."—R.C. Sproul

"Worship is the missing jewel in the evangelical church."—A.W. Tozer

"God has sovereignly pulled back the curtain on His glory. He has disclosed Himself on the platform of both creation and redemption that we might stand awestruck in His presence, beholding the sweet symmetry of His attributes, pondering the unfathomable depths of His greatness, baffled by the wisdom of His deeds and the limitless extent of His goodness. This is His beauty."—Sam Storms

"People imagine that if they attend a religious service, are reverent in their demeanor, join in the singing of the hymns, listen respectfully to the preacher, and contribute to the collection, they have really worshipped God . . . Poor deluded souls, a delusion which is helped forward by the priest-craft and preacher-graft of the day. Over against this delusion are the words of Christ in John 4:24, which are startling in their plainness and pungency: 'God is Spirit; and they that worship Him must worship Him in spirit and in truth.'"—A.W. Pink

"In order to worship God, God must be known: and He cannot be known apart from Christ."—A.W. Pink

"'Worship' is the new nature in the believer stirred into activity, turning to its Divine and heavenly Source. It is that which is 'spirit' (John 3:6) turning to Him who is 'Spirit.'"—A.W. Pink

"Worship is a posture of life that takes as its primary purpose the understanding of what it really means to love and revere God."
—Ravi Zacharias

168 Hours in a Week: Let's Focus One Hour
On Our Savior's Amazing Sacrifice—Together

The following is an illustration to transition us from this chapter on worship into the next chapter on tithing.

G. Campbell Morgan tells of a friend of his who had a little daughter that he dearly loved. They were great friends; the father and daughter were always together. But there seemed to come an *estrangement* on the child's part. The father could not get her company as before and she seemed to be somewhat distant. If he wanted her to walk with him, she always had something else to do.

The father was grieved and could not understand what the trouble was. His birthday came and in the morning his daughter came to his room, her face radiant with love, and handed him a present. Opening the parcel, he found a pair of exquisitely made slippers. The father said, "My child, it was very good of you to buy me such lovely slippers."

"O father," she said, "I did not *buy* them—I *made* them for you!"

Looking at her he said, "I think I understand now, what long has been a mystery to me. Is this what you have been doing for the last three months?"

"Yes," she said, "but how did you know how long I have been at work on them?"

He said, "Because for three months I have missed your company and your love. I have wanted you with me—but you have been *too busy.* These are beautiful slippers—but next time *buy* your present, and let me have *you* all the days. I would rather have my child *herself,* than anything she could *make* for me."

CHAPTER 7

IS THE 10% TITHE 100% MISUNDERSTOOD?

Goal & Purpose:
Most Christians' perception of the word *tithe* is based
on a misunderstanding of Scripture. The Jewish
tithe was always a percentage of *crops and livestock—
never money,* despite the fact that currency was used
and mentioned in Scripture before tithing.
The 10 percent tithe was introduced into mainstream
Protestant denominations around 1895.
Before the twentieth century, tithing for New Testament
Christians was considered to be a false teaching.
Many churches and TV "evangelists" preach
a message that leads their unsuspecting
audience to think that God will bless them
for giving money—claiming that it is a way
to demonstrate or prove one's faith.
As we will see, this is a vestige of
traditionalism and not biblically sound.

*"Each one must give as he has decided in his heart,
not reluctantly or under compulsion, for God loves
a cheerful giver."*—2 Corinthians 9:7

Few subjects today are as misunderstood—and as commonly taught in
a way that is simply not biblical—as tithing. As we open this chapter, I
challenge you to take another look at the Scriptures and question your
assumptions about the 10 percent tithe.

This is from the from the Billy Graham Evangelistic Associations' "Questions and Answers":

"Tithing is not mentioned in the New Testament except where it is describing Old Testament practices or in the Gospels where Jesus is addressing people who were under the Old Testament law. Note Jesus' comments to the Pharisees in Luke 11:42. A New Testament teaching on giving which may be helpful to you is found in 1 Corinthians 16:2 . . . This passage brings out four points: we should give individually, regularly, methodically, and proportionately. The matter of your giving is between you and God, and He always takes into account our circumstances. He knows when they are beyond our power to direct and control. The important thing is that we see *giving as a privilege* and *not a burden.* It should not be out of a *sense of duty,* but rather out of love for the Lord and a desire to see His kingdom advanced. II Corinthians 9:6-7 . . . What has priority in our lives? Is Christ really first—or do we put ourselves and our own desires first? Make sure Christ is first in your life, and then ask Him to guide you."

Some Traditional Views About Tithing

- Tithing is biblical and a duty of those who claim to be Christians.
- Tithing is necessary to support the church.
- Tithing is a means of proving our faith.
- God honors tithing by "blessing" those who tithe.
- The "blessings" are usually financial. (Like returns on an investment)
- Those who give and the amount given are often points of interest to church leaders.

Consider These Points . . .

- God doesn't need our money.
- Tithing is never money or currency in the Bible—it is always from crops or from the spoils of war.
- Currency was used for many things in the OT, but never to pay a tithe.
- The "holy" tithe, as used by Moses, Malachi, and Jesus, was always food from inside God's *holy* land of Israel. Abram's tithe from the spoils of war was a pagan law of the land.
- Tithing ranged from 1 percent to 23.5 percent.
- The Levites who received the tithes in the OT were not allowed to own land but received the tithe in lieu of a land inheritance. They did have other sources of income.
- The nonpriestly Levites gave 10 percent of the tithes they received to the priests. The total that the Levite priests received was 1 percent.
- Giving our money and time to ministries is important—but it's not a "tithe."
- Giving is between ourselves and the Lord.
- Expecting something in return is investing.
- Everything that comes from God is a blessing—including cancer, job loss, car wrecks, etc.
- God loves a cheerful giver. Giving should be done as a reflection of our thankfulness.
- We should consider the importance of staying out of debt so we can give.
- Getting out of debt should be strongly considered before giving.
- Debt-free Christians can freely give much more than those struggling.
- First-expense giving is not biblical—that's a misuse of a biblical text.
- Again, God doesn't need our money—giving is an issue of the heart.
- Giving when it may lower our comfort and lifestyle is good and right.

The Three Tithes According to the Bible

(Again—tithes are never money!)

1) *The Levitical tithe.* Support for the Levitical workers. The workers then supported the priests by giving 1 percent to them. These crops were distributed to the Levitical cities.
2) *The festival tithe.* Crops and food were brought to the streets of Jerusalem during the three major festivals. If you could not comfortably transport your festival tithe to Jerusalem, it could be sold so that currency could easily be carried and then exchanged back into food for the festival. It was to be shared and eaten in the streets of Jerusalem.
3) *The poor tithe.* Used to help the poor among the Israelites. Payable every third year. This tithe (again, a crop) was kept in homes and given as needs arose.

Additional Points to Consider . . .

- Jesus (as a carpenter), Paul (as a tentmaker), and Peter (as a fisherman) were not required to pay tithes.
- Unbiblical teaching about tithing keeps many people away from church.
- Martin Luther, John Calvin, C.S. Lewis, and others warned that the tithe was not for Christians.
- Some Christians give over 90 percent of their incomes. Some give zero. That is between them and God.
- Even financially challenged teachers in the New Testament never endorsed tithing.
- Many proponents of tithing claim the OT was legalistic. Yet they are likely becoming legalistic with this teaching.
- Those who teach tithing for today conveniently hold to tithing while rejecting other aspects of the Old Covenant (Hebrews 8:13).

- What we give (money, time, gifts, etc.) is clearly an issue of the heart and is *not* to be under any compulsion (2 Corinthians 9:7)
- Tithing did not originate with people in the Bible. A tenth was easy math and common in other ancient cultures.
- Paul does much writing about money and giving in chapters 8 and 9 of 2 Corinthians—yet he never mentions tithing.
- Early church ministers relied on gifts from believers. Perhaps this kind of dependency could revolutionize the hearts of pastors and their flocks today (Luke 9:3-5, Luke 10:4-7, and especially Matthew 10:7-10).
- The tabernacle and the ark of the covenant, built by Moses and the people of Israel after leaving Egypt, would cost several million dollars to build today. It was paid for by freewill offerings.
- The temple was built without tithes or taxes.
- After Constantine, magnificent churches were begun, and the persecuted church became respectable. An ecclesiastical system and institutional "church" was forming—with less regard for God's Word. Tithes were established. Tithing was advocated by the Council of Tours in 567 and made civil law in the Carolingian Empire in 765. It remained in England and Wales until the "Tithe Act" in 1936.
- Not a single New Testament Scripture supports tithing as something which Christians should be practicing in our day.
- In Matthew 23:23, Jesus tells us about the hearts of hypocrites in His day. Interestingly, He reminds us that the tithe is crops—yet these men tithed from crops of little value.
- In Luke 18:12, we see again that "New Testament tithing" is mentioned only to reveal self-righteousness.
- The Old Covenant was still in place when Jesus was teaching these things, and He taught the whole law; therefore, He endorsed the tithe to these Jews. See also Matthew 23:23b.
- In Hebrews 7:4-10, we read that Abraham, the patriarch, gave a tenth "of the spoils." This passage is often misused by pastors to say that we should follow the faithfulness of Abraham and do likewise. So next time you overtake a city, make sure you give

a tenth of the spoils. (Reading further into this chapter reveals that the purpose of the tithe from Abraham to Melchizedek was to give him honor.)

- Modern tithing can be, and often is, a chain around a Christian's neck.

- Since God is sovereignly in control and He is the one who determines the failures and successes of our daily efforts, then pastors should rely on His mighty hand—not on some manipulative system to coerce congregations to tithe. *God moves in men's and women's hearts* to support various ministries and missions. *Relaxing in God's sovereignty is beautiful.* The use of tithing as a stratagem to pressure others to give is menacing. Second Corinthians 3:16-17 reminds us, "Nevertheless when one turns to the Lord, the veil is taken away. Now the Lord is the Spirit; and where the Spirit of the Lord is, there is liberty."

As New Testament Christians, we *cannot* give a biblical tithe.

Again, the biblical tithe was crops and animal herds grown and/or raised *by Jews* in Israel and *given to the Levites*.

It was *never expected that non-Jews would tithe.* Jews living outside Israel did not tithe. Jews inside Israel who did not grow or raise food did not tithe (because they had nothing to tithe).

God has given us a New Covenant. Anyone adhering to the Old denies Christ's life, death, and resurrection (Galatians 5:4). Tithing is a part of that Old Covenant.

Giving Is a Privilege—Not an Obligation

While giving is necessary to cover the expenses of churches, missions, and various legitimate ministries, the funds for these should be received as freewill gifts, not tithes. Christians who give as various and legitimate needs are made known ought to be responding to a genuine concern for others. The amount might be 1 percent, 10 percent, or 90 percent. In fact, using a percentage is not even a realistic basis for giving.

Proper giving will originate from:

- Seeing a need that God has placed before you.
- Using common sense and counsel to determine if it's wise to give financial support.
- Determining personal finances before giving. Avoid the false teaching that you are to "pay your tithe" first, then let your debts come second. This idea is not biblical—it is part of an engineered system of conning money out of unsuspecting people, usually the poor and elderly.

"Tithing" carries the connotation of a tax, a duty, or an obligation. There's a subtle, yet important difference between "tithing" and "giving." Paying a tithe, with the sense that it is an obligation, falls right in line with legalism, even if we deny that it is legalism. Paying the church a portion of our income with the thought that it is fulfilling our duty can actually be a sagacious way of trying to prove our worth while claiming that we are trusting in Christ. *This completely misses the point of grace!*

Dr. Russell Earl Kelly, the author of *Should the Church Teach Tithing?*, made some interesting comments during a radio interview. He stated, "This is one of the easiest issues anyone can learn about. There's sixteen verses that talk about the tithe in the Bible. Just open your concordance and read them."

The following is a short summary of Dr. Russell Kelly's conviction:

New Covenant giving is: freewill, sacrificial, generous, joyful, regular and motivated by love for God, fellow Christians and lost souls. Do not burden or curse God's poor who struggle to feed and shelter their family. Although there is no set percentage for Christians to give, all should give sacrificially or lower your standards of living in order to further the reach of the Gospel.

Dr. Kelly's work has been a great inspiration and help and is highly recommended reading for anyone wanting to acquire a thorough biblical understanding of the tithing issue. Dr. Kelly's website is a well-organized, thorough superabundance of convincing information about tithing. It is a tremendous resource: www.Tithing-RussKelly.com.

"So, God—Let's Make a Deal"

Any form of giving, whether it's called a tithe or a freewill offering, that is given with the hope that God will bless the giver and multiply his "investment" is attempting to extort money or blessings from God. Money-hungry preachers, particularly those on television, will tell their audiences that giving is a verification of their faith and that God will bless that faith with a variety of benefits. Certainly the reward will exceed their giving—eventually.

INVESTMENT OR GIFT?

In reality, such a "gift" has now become an investment. It's no longer a gift. More important, this is not biblical—it's nothing short of opportunistic greed by both parties. Many of these so-called "preachers" are really sharks posturing their deceit from a pulpit while claiming to be men of God. These con men disguise themselves with Bibles and expensive suits. Occasionally they will manage to preach some biblical truths. Even the deceiver in the garden of Eden used truth mixed with his own deception when Eve was beguiled. These snake-oil salesmen use the same routine.

Most of the people who are giving money are also in error and oftentimes participating with warped motives. They may be:

1) Giving with hopes of getting something in return.
2) Attempting to prove their faith by giving money.
3) Hoping to win favor with God in some way.

To support such "investment" giving, some will cite verses like Proverbs 3:9-10, which gives us this principle: "Honor the Lord with your wealth, with the first fruits of all your crops; then your barns will be filled to overflowing, and your vats will brim over with new wine."

Keep in mind that this is a *principle,* not a promise. And it certainly does not preclude the New Testament teaching about debt.

Debts and Giving

While many are led to believe that they should give (or pay) their tithe before anything else, this seems clearly adverse to the important biblical teaching on getting out of debt.

Romans 13:8 tells us, "Owe no one anything, except to love each other, for the one who loves another has fulfilled the law." Mortgages and car payments, which are generally fixed monthly living expenses, would probably not be fair to include in Paul's counsel here; however, most of our other debts should be given serious consideration.

As Christians, we should consider the personal problems and pressures of indebtedness. It seems clear that God wants us to "owe no one anything." Consider too the ones to whom the money is owed. *What if we were in their position?* Would we feel it was right for our debtor to "pay a tithe" before paying us back?

Jesus tells us in Matthew 7:12, "So whatever you wish that others would do to you, do also to them, for this is the Law and the Prophets."

Giving "first fruits" after we're out of debt makes much more sense. Don't forget, God doesn't need your money. Giving is a reflection of our thankfulness for what He's already done. It's not a "deal" to show God that you're worthy of His blessings. (*None of us are worthy* of His blessings. What He does for us is because He is merciful and gracious!)

The following verse is profound and important to those who have been redeemed by Jesus.

> "For they gave according to their means, as I can testify, and *beyond their means, of their own accord,* begging us earnestly for the favor of *taking part* in the relief of the saints—and this, not as we expected, but they gave themselves first to the Lord and then by the will of God to us." (2 Corinthians 8:3-5)

The emphasis of Scripture is clear:
Giving to your church—yes!
Support good ministries—yes!

"Each one must give as he has decided in his heart, *not reluctantly or under compulsion,* for God loves a cheerful giver." (2 Corinthians 9:7)

We are undoubtedly called to financially support the local church, as well as to give of our time and efforts. However, that giving is between us and God. It is not an obligation or tithe.

Our motive is key. God wants our hearts—not our money.

Again, God does not need your money.

SUMMARY: As Christians, supporting ministries with our time and finances is an *awesome privilege.* To be a part of ministries that teach God's Word and help those in need is a great thing. However, to give *as an obligation,* especially to fulfill "a tithing obligation," is wrong. Those who promote tithing or any form of compulsory giving are in biblical error.

Quotes Worth Requoting

"But you are not under a system similar to that by which the Jews were obliged to pay tithes to the priests. If there were *any such rule* laid down in the Gospel, it would destroy *the beauty of spontaneous giving* and take away all the bloom from *the fruit of your liberality!* There is no law to tell me what I should give my father on his birthday. There is no rule laid down in any law book to decide what present a husband should give to his wife, nor what token of affection we should bestow upon others whom we love. No, *the gift must be a free one, or it has lost all its sweetness."*—Charles H. Spurgeon

"Again I would remind you that *we are not under the tithe system today.* There are many humble believers with very little income for whom a tenth would be too much to give."—Dr. J. Vernon McGee

"How many marriages deteriorate into empty motions because husbands do not hear the silent yearnings of the wife: 'I don't want your money, I want you.' How many parents have lost their children because they failed to interpret the signs: 'I don't want your presents, Daddy, I want you.'" And *how many tithing churchgoers will be lost to the kingdom* because the word of God never reached their hearts: 'I will seek not what is yours *but you.*'"—John Piper

"God wants your hand before He wants the work of your hand. He wants your heart, before He wants the giving of your heart. *He wants you. And when He gets you—He won't have any issue with you giving as needs arise.*"—Dr. J. Vernon McGee

"In matters pertaining to the giving of money, the grace principle involves the believer's recognition of God's sovereign authority over all that the Christian is and has, and *contrasts* with the Old Testament legal system of tithing."—Lewis Sperry Chafer

"*I do not believe* that Christians today are under the ten percent tithe system. We are not obligated to percentage tithe at all. There is not a single verse in the New Testament where God specifies that we should give ten percent of our income to the church . . . . We are to give as we are able. For some this will mean less than ten percent, but for others whom God has materially blessed, this will mean much more than ten percent."—Ron Rhodes

"The New Testament teaches proportional giving according to what we have, not what we don't have. (II Corinthians 8:12). If we can only give 5% as the Lord leads, so be it. It is not how much you give that matters to God, but the attitude and motive which you are giving from."—Zola Levitt

"We give because it benefits the body of Christ that we are a part of. We give so that the needs of the less fortunate are met and so there could be some level of equality in our midst."—Larry Richards

CHAPTER 8

THE RED CARPET BEFORE
THE MAJESTY OF GRACE

Goal & Purpose:
Perhaps we should consider the importance of
helping others understand the problem
before giving them the answer.
The customary presentation of the gospel
seems to be centered around what God has done for us.
Let's look closely at whether our gospel message
is "man-centered" or "God-centered."

"Proclaim the good news of His salvation from day to day.
Declare His glory among the nations, His wonders among all
peoples. For the Lord is great and greatly to be praised."
—from Psalm 96

In their book *The School of Biblical Evangelism,* Ray Comfort and Kirk
Cameron explain why good news needs to be shared *after* there's an
understanding of the problem:

> The Law is the God-given "key" to unlock the door of salvation.
> The Bible says in Psalm 19:7, "The law of the Lord is perfect
> converting the soul." Scripture makes it very clear that it is the Law
> that actually converts the soul. To illustrate the function of God's
> Law, let's look for a moment at civil law. Imagine if I said to you,
> "I've got some good news for you; someone has just paid a $2,500
> speeding fine on your behalf." You'd probably react by saying,
> "What are you talking about? That's not good news—it doesn't

make sense. I don't have a $2,500 speeding fine." My good news wouldn't be good news to you; it would seem foolish. But more than that, it would be offensive to you, because I'm insinuating you've broken the law when you don't think you have.

However, if I put it this way, it may make more sense: "While you were out today, the law clocked you going 55 miles per hour through an area set aside for a blind children's school. There were ten clear warning signs stating that fifteen miles an hour was the maximum speed, but you went straight through at 55. What you did was extremely dangerous; there's a $2,500 fine. The law was about to take its course, when someone you don't even know stepped in and paid the fine for you. You are very fortunate."

Can you see that telling you precisely what you've done wrong first—actually enables the good news to make sense? If I don't clearly bring understanding that you've violated the law, then the good news will seem foolish and offensive. But once you understand that you've broken the law, then that good news will become good news indeed.

Before the Majestic Presentation

For centuries, royalty and important individuals have been honored with the custom of rolling out a red carpet before they are to be presented. The red carpet is appropriate in that it lets people know that someone worthy of attention is at hand.

The most important message we can present to others is about our God. His majesty and mercy. His holiness and love. The plan He has made known to us that reveals the way He redeems lost sinners and grants forgiveness through the amazing work of His Son on the cross.

However, there should be protocol. Before we present His majesty and the message of His saving kindness, the red carpet should be rolled out.

What is the red carpet?

The red carpet is the foundation laid out before the good news of the gospel.

Essentially, it's the law, or the Ten Commandments. It's also the truth about God's holiness and righteousness compared with who we are. When we accurately understand that we are *not* the good people we may think we are, a truth that becomes apparent when we look into the mirror of the Ten Commandments, it prepares our hearts to see His majesty and the importance of the amazing act Jesus accomplished on the cross.

God uses the Ten Commandments to prepare lost men's attitudes for His message of grace. Most of us have assumed that the Ten Commandments are a set of rules that tell us what we need to do in order to please God. If we take a few minutes to look at them, it's obvious that we have broken them, yet most of us have never properly understood them nor had the hard shells around our hearts broken by seeing the law of God for what it is.

As Charles Spurgeon stated:
"The Law breaks the hard heart.
God's mercy heals the broken heart."

How Are the Ten Commandments a Mirror?

Before you enter an important meeting or interview, you might find a mirror—just to make sure you look good. Check your face or hair. Ensure that your tie is right or take a glimpse to see that you don't have a smudge on your face.

The mirror we have been given by our Creator is the Ten Commandments. Without a mirror, we might not know how we appear. Likewise, God's mirror reveals our hearts.

Romans 3:19 tells us, "By the Law is the knowledge of sin." Again, Paul tells us in Romans 7:7, "I would not have known what sin was except by the Law." The Ten Commandments reveal the truth to us about our position before God as rebels who are spiritually dead.

Paul's Conversion (What he saw)

- Luke tells us three times in the book of Acts about Paul's transformation on the trip to Damascus. Paul, or Saul as he was known before God changed him, was going there to arrest Christians. God blinded him temporarily with a bright light. It seems that Paul used this miraculous transformation as his testimony before hundreds or thousands.
- He was heading in one direction and God turned him. *What he saw changed him.* When others see what has happened to us, that too can be used of God to open their eyes.

A testimony of what God has done in transforming our lives, along with an explanation of the law and the gospel, is evidence to others that may change hearts and minds.

Using the Law . . .

- Helps others to see their problem (not in a condemning manner).
- Lets them know their Holy Creator will hold them accountable.
- Encourages repentance and faith—repent (which means to turn 180 degrees) and believe (like you believe or trust in a parachute).
- Helps individuals to see that they can glorify God by trusting Him and not themselves.

NOTE: www.LivingWaters.com has an excellent eight-part training program called *The Way of the Master* that consists of a series of thirty-minute DVDs followed by questions and discussion. This is a straightforward and simple program for any church, Bible study group, or Sunday school class. Kirk Cameron and Ray Comfort take you to the streets and show dozens of discussions where they help others to see the law and the gospel clearly. It's exciting to hear people thanking them for the clear message.

The Modern Gospel

By contrast, in witnessing we should avoid man's way or "the modern gospel." This usually involves:

- Attempting to get decisions.
- Telling people that God loves them and has a great plan for their life. (He may have a great plan for their life—but that's not the gospel. In fact, coming to Christ may be the beginning of many challenges and difficulties. This notion that God has a "great plan" for every life sounds like people should expect walking with God to be a bed of roses.)
- Encouraging others that all they need to do is make a decision and pray a prayer (sincerely).

WHAT ARE THE TEN COMMANDMENTS FOR?

The Ten Commandments are to show us how bad we are and to show us our need for a Savior. They show us our utter failure in the sight of God. Because they help us to see our sins—we can know we have a problem. *The moral law causes the message of mercy to make sense.* "Because by the works of the Law no flesh will be justified in His sight; for through the Law comes the knowledge of sin."—Romans 3:20

Suppose that you're chatting with a friend or stranger, and you want to share the gospel. You can start with something like this: "I've learned something really interesting that I like to tell others about, and it involves asking a few questions first. Do you mind if I ask you a few questions? I think you'll find them interesting."

Then the questions begin. "Do you consider yourself to be a good person?" (Most people will say yes.) Then you can ask, "Have you ever told a lie?" Then you might add, "If you're *like me,* you have probably told hundreds of lies in your lifetime."

When they admit to having told a lie (as most people will do), you can ask, "Did you know that's a violation of the ninth commandment?"

Next, "Have you ever stolen anything? Even if it was small and no one ever knew about it?" Most people will admit that they are guilty of that one too. It's important to smile and admit something like, "I'm finding out we're a lot alike! That's the eighth commandment. Third question. Have you ever used God's name in vain?"

Most people will admit this, and you can point out that even "OMG" is a form of using God's name wrongly. "Anytime we use His name flippantly or carelessly, it's an offense to Him, and this is a violation of the third commandment.

"So based on these three commandments, and we're not even looking at the other seven—and I can tell you I'm guilty of breaking them all—does it concern you that on judgment day, you would be guilty before our Creator?"

Most people will tell you that it does concern them; however, some will insist that they're not as bad as other people. At that point, you can agree—in fact, you can even let them know that you are probably much more guilty than they are. It's also worth conveying the truth that God doesn't grade us on a curve. James 2:10 tells us, "For whoever keeps the whole law and yet stumbles in one point, he has become guilty of all."

It's very appropriate to ask, "If it concerns you that you would be guilty standing before your Creator and Judge, do you know what God has done so that you can leave that courtroom free and clear from any condemnation?"

Now is the appropriate time to bring in the majesty of the gospel. The red carpet has been laid—and it only took a few minutes to roll it out. Now there's an anticipation in your listener for the answer you're about to explain.

The law not only shows the problem and brings them to admit with their own lips that they are guilty and concerned, but the law also softens the heart. The shell around a sinner's heart is cracked with the revelation of guilt.

Now the gospel makes sense. This isn't just some religious idea; this is the answer to our deepest problem—the sin that separates us from our Creator. The gospel doesn't call us to a system of works. We are called to repent, trust in Christ's finished work, and rest in Him.

Presenting the Majesty of the Gospel

After people have admitted that they are concerned, attentive to the truth that they would be guilty standing before God on judgment day, and you ask, "Do you know what God has done so you won't be guilty?", you can explain what Jesus did. This is much different when you have someone who *wants to know,* because God's law has been used to help them become receptive.

"Jesus came to earth for one primary reason—not to teach or do miracles, which He did, but to die on the cross. That was His plan before creation. He knew we would be desperate sinners, rebellious against God. His Father will not allow sin into Heaven, and we have no way of getting rid of our sin. Jesus's purpose on the cross was to die and shed His blood as payment for my sins and yours.

"If we admit to God that we are guilty and repent, which means to turn 180 degrees—marching away from our sinful life and placing our trust in Him and His amazing sacrifice on the cross—He gives us life eternal.

"You can repent and place your trust in Him by simply telling Him what's going on in your heart. This is the most important thing you will ever do."

At this juncture, you can offer to answer questions and encourage them to take time to think about this. If they want to place their trust in Christ right away or seem receptive to praying with you, be sure to remind them that they have been saved by the repentance and faith that God has given them—not the prayer. You can ask them if they have a Bible at home and encourage them to read it, maybe starting with the Gospel of John or Paul's Letter to the Romans. If you have a Bible study or good church to recommend, that's great.

Following Up

In Matthew 28:19, we are told to make disciples. That means to do more than introduce others to the law and the gospel—discipling involves helping newer Christians understand various truths about God's Word and their new life in Christ. It would be ideal to keep in touch with those we help bring the truth of God's plan of redemption, however, not everyone we talk to will be able to meet with us or someone we know. In these cases, we can give them a good study Bible and maybe some tracts or booklets. Perhaps we can recommend a good church. There are many great websites designed specifically to help answer questions and provide solid teaching to new believers. And with e-mail and cell phones, it is much easier to keep in touch with new people we meet.

An important thought to remember is this: God is sovereignly in command of our encounters. *All our encounters, not some.* When we share the law and the gospel with others, it is because our Savior designs these meetings. If we cannot keep in touch, we can relax knowing that God is in control of their future. We can give Him the glory for the privilege of having met—and the honor of having rolled out the red carpet before presenting the majesty of God's grace and mercy.

NOTE: Some may say that we shouldn't condemn anyone, and they are right. It is helpful and kind to make sure those we speak with on these issues understand that. All the law does is reveal to others that they are "condemned already" (John 3:18). The law shows them the danger they're already facing. Therefore, their desperate need for a Savior is revealed. *We are not condemning anyone.* We are helping to reveal God's Word, showing the truth while admitting that *we too are guilty* of these same sins. Remember, there are only two kinds of people in the world: lost sinners and saved sinners. Saved sinners are saved by God's mercy, not by *anything* of their own.

The Damage that Comes from an Inaccurate Gospel Message

The modern gospel avoids helping the lost see their sin and the seriousness of God's wrath. It is most often presented as a way to improve your life or marriage. Many are led to believe that Jesus provides happiness. Perhaps believing in Jesus will stop their drug or alcohol problem or help them get over past hurts. Sometimes they are told that this will fill the emptiness in their heart and provide peace and joy.

Those who are given such a "gospel" see no need for repentance and faith or forgiveness before a Holy Judge. The seriousness of sin is set aside because we don't want to offend or "turn people off" by talking about sin.

Jesus did not die on the cross to give us happiness. He died as the perfect sacrifice for our sins. He died for the forgiveness of the sins of all those to whom His Father has chosen to give repentance and faith. He died to please His Father—it's all about God's glory, not our happiness. The modern message is a lie because it is inaccurate and incomplete.

Many who buy into the false teaching that Christ brings us fulfillment don't realize they've been ushered in with a series of promises that are not in line with the truth of the gospel. Most fall away from fellowship. Some may stay for the programs and activities, while only a few may be truly saved, having genuine repentance and faith.

The most serious aspect of the false gospel is that it makes people comfortable and content. Ray Comfort has stated, "Those who think they are doing fine need to be confronted with the holy Law that they have violated. Then they will see themselves through the eyes of the Judge of the Universe and will flee to the Savior."

Those who have been given the false gospel—and then fall away—are often so turned off by the whole situation that they become hardened to anyone talking about Jesus or the Bible.

When it comes down to it, it's paramount for us to realize the gravity of our sin because of the One we've sinned against.

Some insist that they've lived a very clean life and will act as though their "few" sins are not such a big deal. We know from God's Word that even the slightest sin makes us a sinner. It's not necessarily the gravity of the offense. It's the fact that our sins are against a holy and perfect God who will not allow any sin into His presence.

If I tell a lie to my little five-year-old daughter, there are really no repercussions. If I tell a lie to my wife, I might be sleeping on the couch. A lie to my boss might get me fired, and if I lie before a congressional hearing in Washington DC, I could end up in prison. All of these have different results, yet they are all equally lies. In the book of Proverbs we are told that God hates the lips that lie. Ultimately, every one of our sins is directly against Him.

The Ultimate Purpose of the Law

The law is the thundering voice of God condemning mankind. Should God not hate us? We have offended Him in serious ways! Yet, with all our rebellion, He has been patient with us. Don't be misled into thinking that your sins are no big deal or that you're no worse than most others.

Isn't the law of God enough to convince you of your sin? By God's Spirit and the work of your own conscience, don't you know you are guilty? If we see these commandments and know we are guilty, then they have been a very useful influence on us by showing us the danger we face.

When we see our danger with the opportunity to flee, why would we not run? We should desire to jump from this fiery, sinking ship into the kind, outstretched arms of a Savior.

The law reveals more than words. It reveals what's deep in the heart of each and every person. When God's Word says, "You shall not commit adultery," it means more than the physical act. Jesus said, "He who looks upon a woman with lust has committed adultery with her already in his heart" (Matthew 5:28).

Our hearts are guilty, and God wants our hearts. He wants us to be humble. When we understand and admit our guilt and *see His provision for our forgiveness—He wins our hearts!*

If God Is Sovereign, Why Should I Be Concerned About Telling Others About Him?

Since God is sovereign over everything and we know that He has sovereignly chosen those He is bringing to redemption, why should we make an effort to witness? Why not just sit back and do nothing? After all, if God is going to bring certain people to Himself, why does He need me?

There are many reasons!

1) We are commanded to go into all the world. See Mark 16:15 and Matthew 28:19-20. First Peter 3:15 reminds us to do this with kindness and humility.
2) We share the gospel to edify others. Whether we are sharing some new revelation or truth God has shown us with other believers or nonbelievers, our witness gives glory and praise to God. See Romans 14:19, Hebrews 10:25, and Ephesians 4:29.
3) It should be a natural aspect of our excitement. When a newsworthy event happens, we bring it up in water-cooler discussions. When something really exciting happens to us, we find ways of including it in our day-to-day conversations. Important areas of what God has done or is currently doing in your life should be shared in a genuine and informal manner.
4) It invigorates or boosts other Christians. Oftentimes, when we seek to shift a worldly conversation to something spiritual, we might discover another Christian! Finding another Christian allows you both to talk about your Savior.
5) It's a great way to show genuine kindness, which is certainly a worthy reflection of what Jesus has done for us.

We are allowed the joy of seeing God bring people to Himself. If we are the instrument He uses, what more of a thrill could we ask for?

> "Evangelism and missions are not imperiled
> by the *Biblical truth of election,* but empowered
> by it, and their triumph is secured by it"
> —John Piper

102

What We See Changes Us

Try to imagine that you are leaving one of the World Trade Center buildings on the morning of September 11, 2001—ten minutes before the first building collapses. Suddenly the horrendous sound and screams increase, and you turn to look back two blocks as that huge building sinks downward. The huge plume of dust overwhelms you. This is a sight that you will never forget. What you have seen and experienced will vividly remain with you for the rest of your life.

When we stand in a place of understanding our predicament before our Holy Creator, realizing that we have a serious problem and then turning to see His precious Son on that cross, covered in blood and lifeless—that sight makes an impact that will stay with us throughout eternity. Knowing that He planned this trip to our world to die as the perfect lamb. Knowing that He did this so that we could have forgiveness of our sins, and that He would impute His righteousness to us, the worthy for the unworthy. *Seeing this changes everything.*

SUMMARY: There are various ways to introduce the important message of God's plan of redemption for the lost. In our society, probably more than in previous generations, the use of a few questions based on the law can be the bright light that gains someone's attention. It's just like Paul's encounter on the road to Damascus: *what he saw changed him forever!* When a lost sinner sees himself in light of the law, perhaps this will be the way God *breaks his hardened heart.* Seeing Jesus clearly as the One who came and died to provide forgiveness *will heal that very same heart.*

As we come to a close of this chapter, we need to consider one last point.

The Gospel Is Not about Me

Our theology needs to be changed from the "me-centered" message which is dominant in our churches today to a truly "God-centered" theology.

The following are common lines we hear regarding the gospel message of our day. Notice the use of the word "you":

- God loves you and wants a relationship with you.
- You sinned and separated yourself from God.
- Jesus died for your sins so that you could have a relationship with God.
- If you believe in Jesus and confess your sins, He will forgive you, and you will spend an eternity in Heaven with Him.

You, you, you. Me, me, me.

It's no wonder so many today like to use these lines. They certainly appeal to the selfish side of man's nature. But the gospel is not about me. The gospel is about God.

The Bible makes it very clear that God is the center of the gospel. He is the One to be showcased.

In Max Lucado's book, *It's Not About Me,* he states:

He told Moses: "By those who come near Me I must be regarded as holy; and before all the people I must be glorified" (Leviticus 10:3 NKJV)

Why did He harden Pharaoh's heart? "I will harden Pharaoh's heart, and he will pursue them [the Israelites]. But I will gain glory for myself through Pharaoh and all his army, and the Egyptians will know that I am the Lord" (Exodus 14:4 NIV).

Why do the heavens exist? The heavens exist to "declare the glory of God" (Psalm 19:1 NIV).

And Jesus declared His mission a success by saying, "I have brought you glory on earth by completing the work you gave me to do" (John 17:4 NIV).

God has one goal: GOD. "I have my reputation to keep up" (Isaiah 48:11 MSG).

So many of the testimonies we hear in church are about the ways people's lives have changed since coming to Christ. There are so many stories about broken lives before God changed them. And it's certainly great to hear about changed lives—but that's still not what the gospel is all about.

It's rare to hear about our amazing Savior and our sovereign God. *So often the conversation is about our lives, with little mention or attention actually given to God.*

After reading Lucado's book *It's Not About Me,* I made an attempt to focus my thoughts and life (and theology) in a more God-centered direction. With day-to-day problems and issues, I attempted to bring the conviction of God's character and sovereignty to the forefront of my thoughts. It's not easy. However, it is a habit worth developing, even over the course of many years.

> The dichotomy that struck me as I began to establish this habit was that every time I went to God's Word with the idea of seeing Scripture in a God-centered fashion, it was His Word that kept bringing *me* back into the scene. While I was trying to be God-centered in my thinking, His Word kept dragging me back into the picture. But what a difference it is to read the Bible looking for Him and *then* see the ways *He brings us* into the story!

As we make a conscious attempt to study God's Word with a God-centered attitude, He is the one who keeps bringing us back into the setting. It's an interesting phenomena: when we focus on Him, we see the amazing ways God includes us.

Quotes Worth Requoting

"The good news is not good news until the bad news is understood." —R.C. Sproul

"The Law breaks the hard heart. God's mercy heals the broken heart."—Charles H. Spurgeon

"It is obvious from Scripture that God requires us not only to preach to sinners, but also to teach them. The servant of the Lord must be 'able to teach, patient in meekness and instruction' to those who oppose them (II Timothy 2:24, 25). For a long while I thought I was to leap among sinners, scatter the seed, then leave. But our responsibility goes further. We are to bring the sinner to a point of understanding his need before God. Psalm 25:8 says, 'Good and upright is the Lord; therefore will He teach sinners in the way.' Psalm 51:13 states, 'Then will I teach transgressors your ways; and sinners shall be converted to you.'"—Ray Comfort

"When preaching and private talk are not available, you need to have a tract ready . . . Get good striking tracts, or none at all. But a touching gospel tract may be the seed of eternal life. Therefore, do not go out without your tracts."—Charles H. Spurgeon

At the age of eighty-two, John Newton, who composed "Amazing Grace," said, "My memory is nearly gone, but I remember two things: that I am a great sinner and that Christ is a great Savior."

"Christ did not die to forgive sinners who go on treasuring anything above seeing and savoring God. And people who would be happy in Heaven if Christ were not there, will not be there. The gospel is not a way to get people to Heaven; it is a way to get people to God. It's a way of overcoming every obstacle to everlasting joy in God. If we don't want God above all things, we have not been converted by the gospel."—John Piper

WE HAVE BEEN ENTRUSTED WITH
THE GREATEST MESSAGE OF ALL

CHAPTER 9

WRONG REASONS TO BELIEVE THE BIBLE

Goal & Purpose:
Many of us assume the Bible is to be taken as truth
because it is culturally sanctioned. My hope is that we will see
the fallacy of using general acceptance as a reliable basis for
believing the Bible and establish for ourselves a cogent
rationale that will stand up to any and all scrutiny.

When asked, "Why do you believe in the Bible?", these are some
common answers:

1) "My parents believe in the Bible, and that's what I was taught."
2) "It changed my life."
3) "My preacher told me that it was true."
4) "It's been the best-selling book in the world for years. It's got
   to be true."
5) "It just seems right. I'm comfortable with it."
6) "I choose to believe it."

None of these are adequate in making a case for the legitimate and
unique value of the Bible, especially on a debate stage or in a courtroom.
In fact, these reasons easily fall into the category of traditionalism, which
again, is believing something because it is culturally acceptable.

If these reasons were a sufficient and reasonable basis for trusting
in a particular writing, then many religious books in the world would
qualify. Certainly there are men and women who could honestly tell you
that the Book of Mormon changed their lives or claim that following

the Quran brought them out of alcoholism. Perhaps the Quran helped them with some other problem or gave them peace. However, there are excellent reasons to believe in the Bible's unique value and character as the Word of God. In this chapter, we'll explore those reasons.

Legitimate Reasons to Believe the Bible

Voddie Bauchum said it well when he answered his Oxford professor as to why he cited the Bible so often and powerfully:

> "The Bible is a RELIABLE COLLECTION of HISTORICAL DOCUMENTS written by eyewitnesses during the lifetime of other eyewitnesses. Their REPORT is of SUPERNATURAL EVENTS which took place as FULFILLMENT of SPECIFIC PROPHECIES and declare that their record is divine in nature and not human in origin."

It can be added that various fields of science, including archaeology, biology, meteorology, oceanography, geology, and anthropology, along with recognized historical writings, show the Bible to be entirely *unique* and *trustworthy*. Its sixty-six books were composed in three languages by more than forty writers on three different continents over a period of fifteen hundred years, yet the message of God's plan to redeem lost sinners is consistent from beginning to end.

No other writing can assert any claims close to these.

These reasons warrant our attention and certainly help us to see that the Bible is unique.

Consider too, the philosophical reasons the Bible makes sense in the flowchart contained in appendix B in this book. This chart helps show the reasonableness of the Bible's worldview and its unique quality as it is compared to other writings in the world.

What About the Quran, the Book of Mormon, the Four Vedas, the Bhagavad Gita, the Pahlavi Texts, Etc.?

The majority of the other religious writings around the world would qualify as legitimate revelations of God if they could meet the standards set by the Bible. Most are a combination of prose and proverbs mixed with various narratives promoting a variety of philosophies. The qualifying criteria that these other writings fail to possess are:

1) Prophecies and the fulfillment of those prophecies
2) Proven historicity
3) Multiple eyewitness accounts
4) Supernatural events consistent with the message
5) Multiple authorship, yet uniformity
6) Ability to reveal scientific facts before science understands them
7) Consistency and comprehensibility
8) A clear revelation of God and His attributes
9) Miraculous assembly and protection
10) A message that declares our purpose and future
11) A message that is beyond the most brilliant, intricate, imaginative, and elaborate team of writers
12) Manuscript evidence. Oldest documents matching newer documents

Prophecy: The Red Silver Dollar

The prophecies of the Bible are amazing, and they rank at the top of the list of reasons to treat the Bible as different from any other book. The very idea of foretelling the future—with amazing detail, as the Bible does—is astounding. This subject should not be taken lightly. Consider how unlikely it is that anything could be described in detail years, decades, or centuries in advance.

While talking to a woman who was reading through the Quran as a promise to her mother, who had just died, I asked if she knew how many prophecies in the Bible had been fulfilled by the birth and life of

Jesus. Her reply was, "What's a prophecy?" After an explanation, she was surprised to find out the Quran only has one specific prophecy. It was Mohammed's prediction that he would return to Mecca—a prophecy he very easily fulfilled himself.

Mark Cahill's book *One Heartbeat Away* uses the analogy of a single red silver dollar getting thrown into a mix of billions of silver dollars three feet deep, enough to cover the state of Texas.

> "What do you think the probability is for you to go blindfolded, wander across Texas for several days, then reach down and pick up that single red coin from the three foot deep ocean of silver dollars?"

Jesus fulfilled over three hundred prophecies in His life. Most of these He could not influence or control from a human perspective, such as where He was born or the fact that soldiers would cast lots for His belongings at His crucifixion.

> "IF Jesus fulfilled *only eight* of these prophecies, it would be comparable to you finding that red silver dollar on your first attempt."

There have been nonbiblical claims of fulfilled prophecy which have gained attention, such as Nostradamus's predictions. However, they are vague, and none of these have the details which the biblical prophecies contain.

One-hundred-percent accuracy in foretelling the future is by far the most revealing and extraordinary requirement of divine origin—*and only the Bible qualifies.*

Prophecies Surrounding the City of Tyre

Josh McDowell, as an atheist and college student, set out to write a convincing volume of texts to disprove the authenticity of the Bible and the deity of Jesus. Several years into the process, God brought him out of his blindness and revealed to him the reliability of the Bible.

After giving his life to Christ, he began to document his findings in various books. One of his earlier works, *Evidence That Demands a Verdict,* presents many areas of science and philosophy, detailing the legitimacy of anyone making the claim that the Bible is entirely unique and trustworthy.

One of the hundreds of biblical prophecies that Josh goes into detail to explain involves the cities of Sidon and Tyre. The prophecy regarding Tyre was written around 580 BC, and it is recorded in Ezekiel 26. Tyre was an ancient city of the Phoenicians, appearing for the first time in Joshua 19 during the reigns of David and Solomon. It was also the commercial center of the Mediterranean.

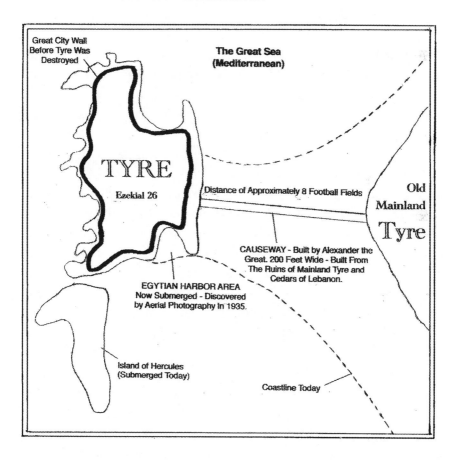

The prophecies concerning it, from the twenty-sixth chapter of Ezekiel, are:

v. 3: Many nations would be against Tyre.

v. 4: The city would become a bare rock, flat like the top of a rock.

v 5: Fishermen would use the area to spread their nets to dry.

v. 8: Nebuchadnezzar would destroy the mainland city of Tyre.

v. 12: The debris of the city's destruction would be thrown into the water.

v. 14: Tyre would never be rebuilt.

What actually happened is an incredible fulfillment of every prophecy. The *Encyclopedia Britannica* records, "After a thirteen year siege by Nebuchadnezzar II, Tyre made terms and acknowledged Babylonian suzerainty. In 538 B.C. Tyre, with the rest of Phoenicia, passed to the suzerainty of Achaemenid Persia." When Nebuchadnezzar destroyed the gates to enter Tyre, he found the city virtually empty. The people had moved by ship to the island offshore about one half-mile. They had strengthened it and remained there for many decades, resisting attacks by numerous other nations.

Alexander the Great came about two hundred years later. He had virtually conquered the world, yet the island city of Tyre remained. After his destruction of the rebuilt portions of mainland Tyre, his army used stones and wood beams to help construct a mole (land bridge) in order to reach the occupied island. This two-hundred-yard-wide effort was extremely dangerous for the workers as the Tyrians would shoot arrows and catapult stones from the fortress walls surrounding the island. Their strategic raids on the causeway project severely retarded progress.

However, Alexander's army was able to finally complete the project, along with two huge towers armed with weapons capable of launching destruction over the city's walls. His navy had grown, with Sidon, Aradus, and Byblus contributing about eighty ships, ten more ships from Rhodes, three more from Soli and Mallos, ten from Lycia, and a large ship from Macedon. Another 120 ships from Cyprus accounted for an overwhelming attack on the little island. It is recorded that eight thousand Tyrians were killed and thirty thousand sold into slavery.

Tyre actually recovered quickly after Alexander, and eighteen years later was again destroyed by Antigonus in 314 BC. Smaller forms of the city either on the spot or close by have been built and then destroyed many times during the last 2500 years. However, it has never been rebuilt as the city it once was.

The current city of Tyre, built a short distance down the coast from the original city, has small fishing vessels at anchor. The port has become a haven for fishing boats and a place for spreading nets, which can be seen virtually every day.

Some skeptics have said the city of Tyre could not be rebuilt if the biblical prophecy was to be truly fulfilled. In actuality, the great city of Tyre has *not* been rebuilt. Tyre would have been the New York City or Los Angeles of its day. Nothing to compare has been rebuilt, even near there.

It's important to remember that the prophecy distinctly states in verse 14, "And I will make you a bare rock; you will be a place for the spreading of nets. You will be built no more, for I the Lord have spoken." In order for fishing nets to be spread, there need to be fishermen and a city to support and justify their occupation. Nina Nelson, after visiting Tyre, stated, "I went to visit Tyre on a summer's day. The town was sleepy, the harbor still. Fishing boats were putting out to sea. Pale turquoise fishing nets were drying on the shore."

Floyd Hamilton has stated, "The old Tyre today sits as it has for twenty-five centuries, a bare rock, uninhabited by man. Today anyone who wants to see the site of the old city, can have it pointed out to him along the shore, but there is not a ruin to mark the spot. It has been scraped clean and has never been rebuilt."

Amazingly, the freshwater springs of Reselain are believed to be pouring millions of gallons of freshwater into the sea at the area of the original Tyre, yet the city has not been rebuilt there. The causeway still remains, and the debris which Alexander's army placed in the water is still visible through the surrounding waters.

Conclusion About Tyre

In the case of Tyre, each of the specific prophecies took place. We have writings that prove the prophecies were written before the events. The writings did not come afterward in order to appear as prophecies.

Archaeological discoveries and historical documents prove that Tyre was a real city and these things really did happen. There is no debate on this. The only debate is whether the prophecy in verse 21 regarding Tyre's "not being found again" has been thwarted by the building of modern-day Tyre.

Peter Stoner has summarized it well: "If Ezekiel had looked at Tyre in his day and had made these seven predictions in human wisdom, these estimates mean that there would have been only one chance in 75,000,000 of their all coming true. They all came true in the minutest detail."

Other Cities and Prophecy

There are hundreds of prophecies to study and several interesting ones regarding cities similar to Tyre. Hosea 13 and Micah 1 contain specific prophecies about the city of Samaria. Biblical and other extant historical documents have shown the prophecies to have been fulfilled in detail.

Sidon, the sister city of Tyre, had its history written in Ezekiel 28:22-23 *before* the horrible and bloody events it experienced. Sidon was different from Tyre in many ways. For one, God did not specify that it would be wiped out and destroyed permanently. It was rebuilt over and over for centuries—only to be continually devastated. No prophecy of extinction was foretold for Sidon, and it continued on. It also has one of the bloodiest histories of any city in the world.

George Davis concludes that, "No human mind could have foretold 2,500 years ago that Tyre would be extinct, and Sidon would continue, but suffer tribulation during the succeeding centuries; instead of Tyre enduring sorrows, and Sidon being desolate and deserted during the long period."

The cities of Gaza and Ashkelon and the small kingdoms of Moab and Ammon have similar prophecies detailed in Scripture. Again, historical data coupled with archaeology have proven these prophecies to have been fulfilled. Prophecies about cities stretch into the New Testament too. We know through prophecy that Bethlehem, the city of David, would be the birthplace of the Messiah and that Jesus would be taken to Egypt and then return (see Micah 5:1-2 and Hosea 11:1).

This is a mere, tiny glimpse of the fascinating study of prophecies in the Bible which have already been fulfilled. Specific and fulfilled prophecies exist in no other book.

The Dead Sea Scrolls and Their Significance

In early 1947 near the Qumran area, better known today as the West Bank, a shepherd boy looking for a lost goat on the northwest shore of the Dead Sea tossed a rock into a cave. He heard the sound of breaking pottery, so he had his cousin help him enter the cliff-side opening. No goat was found, but he did locate the greatest archaeological discovery of all time.

Within the sealed pottery, many ancient writings had been hidden for at least 1,900 years. Several were in excellent condition and some were in disrepair. For over sixty years the ones that were in fragments have been put back together, and they have revealed much about the people who lived in the region two thousand years ago.

The most important thing the Dead Sea Scrolls have revealed is that the books of the Old Testament have not changed in the centuries since they were written. Many were complete copies of the entire Old Testament, except the book of Esther.

Of the four languages used in the scrolls, one is an ancient form of Hebrew that is well over 2,500 years old. The written form of that language has not been used since the days of King David and Solomon. Those recorded words match our Bibles today.

Other manuscripts were also found in at least ten other surrounding caves. Every writing that is related to Scripture has substantiated the Bibles we have been printing since the Gutenberg press, further proof that God's Word has been protected from mistransliteration through the ages.

Apologetics

The systematic use of information to explain the reasonableness of a position is known as apologetics. It is not the art of apologizing. The term developed in the second and third centuries when Christian writers explained their faith to skeptics and those unfamiliar with Christian teachings. First Peter 3:15 is often cited by those who find the science of apologetics fascinating and worthwhile: "But in your hearts set apart Christ as Lord. Always be prepared to give an answer [defense, or *apologia]* to everyone who asks you to give the reason for the hope that you have. But do this with gentleness and respect."

There are volumes of great books, wonderful organizations, and websites devoted to the field of apologetics.

This book's intended focus is to reveal traditionalist views in contrast to Scripture; therefore, a very limited amount of information regarding the unique and scientific characteristics of the Bible can be presented here. Appendix F will reference some additional resources.

SUMMARY: At the beginning of this chapter is a list of at least twelve qualifying criteria that we should probably consider when determining whether the Bible is unique and legitimate as the infallible Word of God. The bulk of this chapter has presented only a tiny glimpse at the first one on the list. Volumes have been written on each of the twelve areas mentioned.

Some readers may contend that their traditionalist reason for believing the Bible is all they need. However, they should consider the fact that there are strong reasons to believe in the Bible's infallibility which can stand up to the skeptics' contentions. Voddie Bauchum's answer might be worth memorizing: "The Bible is a RELIABLE COLLECTION of HISTORICAL DOCUMENTS written by eyewitnesses during the lifetime of other eyewitnesses. Their REPORT is of SUPERNATURAL EVENTS which took place as FULFILLMENT of SPECIFIC PROPHECIES and declare that their record is divine in nature and not human in origin."

My hope is that this chapter will whet your appetite and make it clear that there are solid, empirical reasons to trust in the Bible as God's single, special revelation. It has been given to us and protected through the centuries by His sovereign hand.

Quotes Worth Requoting

"This Book had to be written by one of three people: good men, bad men or God. It couldn't have been written by good men because they said it was inspired by the revelation of God. Good men don't lie and deceive. It couldn't have been written by bad men because bad men would not write something that would condemn themselves. It leaves only one conclusion. It was given by divine inspiration of God."—John Wesley

"As I have dealt with one apparent discrepancy after another and have studied the alleged contradictions between the Biblical record and the evidence of linguistics, archaeology, or science, my confidence in the trustworthiness of Scripture has been repeatedly verified and strengthened."—Dr. Gleason Archer

"It may be stated categorically that no archaeological discovery has ever controverted a Biblical reference. Scores of archaeological findings have been made which confirm in clear outline or exact detail historical statements in the Bible. And, by the same token, proper evaluation of Biblical description has often led to amazing discoveries."—Dr. Nelson Glueck

"For thousands of years most people believed the earth was flat and were afraid of traveling too far lest they would fall off the edge. This was taught by Hindu and Buddhist scripture. Columbus trusted Isaiah 40:22 which states: 'He sits enthroned above the circle of the earth.' He was not afraid of sailing off the edge. Like Columbus, we too can sail into the unknown with the assurance that God's word is true."—www.PleaseConvinceMe.org

"To be skeptical of the resultant text of the New Testament books is to allow all of classical antiquity to slip into obscurity, for no documents of the ancient period are as well attested bibliographically as the New Testament."—John Warwick Montgomery

"The Bible is supported by archaeological evidence again and again. On the whole, there can be no question that the results of excavation have increased the respect of scholars for the Bible as a collection of historical documents."—Millar Burrows

"The Hittites were once thought to be a Biblical legend, until their capital and records were discovered at Bogazkoy, Turkey. It was once claimed there was no Assyrian king named Sargon as recorded in Isaiah 20, because this name was not known in any other record. Then, Sargon's palace was discovered in Khorsabad, Iraq. The very event mentioned in Isaiah 20, his capture of Ashdod, was recorded on the palace walls. What is more, fragments of a stone idol memorializing the victory were found at Ashdod itself."—*Biblical Archeology Magazine*

"Be careful also in your quest for factuality in your study of the Bible. Facts can be used of God to enlighten us, but facts can become an end in themselves and *addict us to being right* and knowing more, or more accurately, than the next guy. WOW, you have no idea how seductive Biblical knowledge can be. *Don't equate facts with truth.* Christ is the truth, and there are a lot of dear brothers whose factual knowledge is minimal, but who know Christ intimately."—John R. Gavazzoni

"Historic figures have homes to visit for posterity; the Lord of history left no home. Luminaries leave libraries and write their memoirs; He left *one book,* penned by ordinary people. Deliverers speak of winning through might and conquest; He spoke of a place in the heart."—Ravi Zacharias

Before Reading Chapter 10 . . .

How would you describe yourself?

With regards to the issue of Hell and eternal conscious agony . . .

1) I believe in the endless agony and torment of the lost. I have no misgivings or reservations about this view.

2) I believe in the eternal agony of the lost. I have no misgivings about this concept and actually look forward to being in Heaven with the knowledge that others will be in Hell experiencing endless torment. I relish the opportunity to see eternal smoke rising from Hell.

3) I believe in the eternal agony of the lost. I honestly have misgivings and discomfort about the idea of eternal torment—but I accept this doctrine because it's been taught by people I trust and it seems to be biblical.

4) I'm not sure what I believe about the eternal destiny of the lost, but I tend to lean toward the idea of eternal torment and conscious pain for those in Hell because that is what I've been led to believe by those in the church.

5) I'm not sure what I believe about the eternal destiny of the lost, but I'm certainly open-minded to whatever the Bible says.

6) I've always had some misgivings about eternal torment and agony for the lost. I'm not sure what I believe about this, and I'm open-minded to what the Bible teaches. It would be a relief to find out that the Bible teaches something different. This doctrine has never seemed consistent with the character of God.

7) I have been taught that Hell is eternal, conscious pain for the unsaved—however, I cannot accept this idea whether the Bible teaches it or not.

8) I believe that Hell is horrible and real and that those who have not been saved will go there. However, I do not believe it is

eternal torture. Since it is described as fire, I believe that it is a place of finality and total destruction.

9) Other: _____

_____

_____

Weigh the evidence.

CHAPTER 10

RETHINKING WHAT WE'VE
BEEN TAUGHT ABOUT HELL

Goal & Purpose:
As a former traditionalist concerning the question
of whether the ultimate destiny of the lost is eternal,
unending conscious agony *or* complete destruction,
my goal is to explain why it seems clear that the Bible
does not support the teaching of everlasting torture.
I also intend to show through many scriptural
texts that man's default setting is not immortality,
as most of us have been led to believe.
Immortality is granted *only* to those who have
placed their confidence and trust in Jesus Christ
and His finished work on the cross.
Immortality is conditional, thus the term *conditionalism.*

The traditional view that Hell is eternal torment is so deeply engrained in our culture that many Christians will recoil at the very idea of questioning this doctrine. In fact, my reaction two years ago to the first Christian who told me that he believed Hell was a place of destruction—not torture—was that he must belong to a cult or be off his rocker.

One year later, I took a serious look at the biblical evidence.
I'm thoroughly convinced that most traditionalists have not done this.
The following evidence deserves your attention.
My hope is that you will make an honest and
serious review of this important subject.

If I'm right, you will be thankful you took the time to do this.
If I'm wrong, you will have not wasted your time because you will
have been studying God's Word and become stronger in your beliefs.

The traditional view about Hell—that it is a place of eternal, conscious torment where lost sinners will forever subsist—needs to be evaluated by every Christian. It is the position that most are led to believe and the one I accepted all my life—until I took another look at the Scriptures.

It has been my relief to join the growing number of conservative and Reformed Christians now declaring that the traditionalist view is wrong. Briefly, Hell is real. Hell is biblical, and it is horrible. However, it is not endless torture. Man's default setting is not to live forever unless God grants him that immortality.

One theologian who has devoted himself to a focused study of this topic for over forty years has stated:

"One issue alone divides traditionalists and conditionalists: Does Scripture teach that God will make the wicked immortal, to suffer unending conscious torment in Hell? Or, does the Bible teach that the wicked will finally and truly die, perish, and become extinct forever, through a destructive process that encompasses whatever degree and duration of conscious torment God might sovereignly and justly impose in each individual case?"

The overwhelming weight of biblical texts that deal with the mortality (or immortality) of man and the surrounding issues pertaining to Hell favor the view that will be presented in this chapter. This viewpoint is sometimes referred to as *annihilationism, conditionalism,* or *conditional immortality.*

For the most part my use of the term *annihilationism* will be rare, simply because it is confusingly associated with groups such as the Jehovah's Witnesses and Christadelphians. It should be made clear that the sentiment presented here *does not support the idea that the lost are annihilated immediately after their physical death here on Earth.* My understanding of Scripture is that the unsaved will be resurrected at judgment day, then destroyed in Hell after an unknown degree of punishment. They are eternally punished—which is destruction. Eternal punishment is not an unending conscious *life* of torture.

It might be noted that the ultimate penalty in Scripture has always been *death*—never torture. Nowhere do we see a biblical precedent for mental or physical abuse or protracted torment as punishment for sin. After coming to an accurate understanding of this long-standing *disparagement of God's character* and plan for the lost, you will probably agree that the traditional view is horrific, awful, gruesome, loathsome, monstrous, sickening, and detestable.

Fortunately, it's not true.

Some of the terms used in this chapter to describe the traditional view of Hell may seem harsh or extreme; however, these expressions come directly from the writings of those who support it. The end of this chapter contains quotes by some of those who have promoted this view. Their words are shocking.

Critics of conditionalism may declare that these descriptions are actually accurate because Hell is a horrible place. It is true—Hell will be a horrible place, and those who will face it prior to their destruction will gnash their teeth in disgust at their God. That is the glaring truth. But the biblical evidence is overwhelming that this period of punishment after judgment will lead to destruction—*not eternal life* in agony and pain.

Before continuing, it might be helpful to consider these seven points:

1) Our understanding of Hell needs to be based 100 percent on the Bible, *not* on the comments of theologians, pastors, or our own emotions. (A great deal of the traditional views we hold are because we are not using our Bibles enough. Most of us tend to rely on those we have grown to trust, and they may be wrong.)

2) Consider how much time you have personally studied this subject. Many Christians who hold to the traditional view cannot honestly say they have devoted even one hour to researching it.

3) Those who have led you to believe that Hell is eternal torment for the lost have probably not devoted themselves to a serious and open-minded study of this subject either. They too may have the stranglehold of traditionalism so tightly around their necks that they can't see the truth, as J.I. Packer says (see his comments in the preface of this book).

4) Keep in mind that biblical truth is not based on the number of people who believe something. Accurate theology is not democratic. However, *the number of highly respected theologians coming out on the side of conditionalism is swiftly increasing* (see appendix E.)

5) Some cults have similar beliefs regarding Hell, but that should not keep us from taking a thorough, open-minded look at what the Bible really says about this important subject. Most cults hold to many orthodox doctrines. That does not necessarily mean those areas of belief are wrong.

6) Even though some traditionalists have sought to defend their views on eternal agony and torment of the lost, they often will *misrepresent the actual views* held by conditionalists. In fact, most traditionalists whom I have researched (and they are many) have mischaracterized and attempted to disparage the views presented by most conditionalists. Imperiously, they *rarely* address the full range of concerns at hand.

7) Keep in mind the fact that this subject has an influence on what we think about our God and how we describe Him to others. If Scripture does not teach that the lost will be eternally tortured, *then we are telling others a horrible lie about our Creator.*

Do you think this is important?

Consider this analogy: After returning home from an evening out with his wife, a man pays the babysitter for watching their five-year-old daughter. When they go upstairs to check on the little girl, they find her awake and crying. After they ask her what is wrong, she tells them that the babysitter told her that if she was not good, her father would cut off her fingers, cut out her heart, and put her in the microwave until she popped.

The man asks his wife, "Why would the babysitter say such a sickening thing?"

Obviously, the babysitter was misrepresenting the father in a horrible manner. Likewise, we too can be guilty of promoting a shocking and vile misrepresentation about our God if the Bible does not really teach the concept of everlasting and unending torture.

What is the traditionalist's view of Hell?

Hell is a place of unending, eternal, conscious, agonizing punishment of the bodies, minds, and souls of the lost. Most believe this involves both darkness and fire.

What is the conditionalist's view of Hell?

Hell is real, and it is horrible. It will be the fire that destroys and consumes after the final judgment. It could involve various degrees of punishment which we do not know. However, Hell will be destroyed, and the smoke of its "forever" fire will last as long as God sovereignly determines it to endure. (When we read Scripture, we must understand that "forever" is a biblical term that is relative—as we see it to mean a period of time as short as three days in Jonah 2:6.) The compelling weight of Scripture supports this view.

The overwhelming weight of social pressure within the church supports the view of unending, everlasting torture. But the Bible passages that address the destiny of the lost consist of terms and descriptions such as *destruction, perishing, death, burnt up, utter loss, gone, cessation,* and many others, as we will see later in this chapter.

Something to Consider

Ask yourself, "Are my beliefs the result of what's been taught by others? Or can I honestly say that my beliefs have been the result of an open-minded, in-depth study of what the Bible says on this subject?"

Rethinking What We've Been Taught About Hell: A Verse-by-Verse Study Through the Bible

For your consideration, the following seventy-one Scriptures clearly lay out what the Bible really teaches about the destiny of the lost, the mortality of man, and the nature of eternal punishment. Appendix F lists the same verses in biblical order. May your study yield a truly biblical understanding.

1. John 3:16: "For God so loved the world that He gave His only Son, that whosoever believes in Him should not perish but have eternal life."

Note the *contrast.* This verse clearly shows us that the antonym to eternal life is to perish. While some might argue that "perish" could mean eternal agony, Jesus did not say "eternal life in Hell"; He used a term that implies finality. If all souls are immortal, why does Jesus speak of eternal life as an option in contrast to death? If the lost burn unendingly for eternity, then God is also giving them eternal life. Despite the fact it would be a horrible life, *it would still be eternal life.*

2. Romans 6:23: "For the wages of sin is *death,* but the free gift of God is *eternal life* in Christ Jesus our Lord."

Again, note the contrast of "death" with "eternal life." Not "eternal, unending life in agony." Death is the result of sin, and the opposite possibility to eternal life is death—not eternal life someplace different. *If we are to believe in a conscious existence of torment, then we are saying eternal life exists for those who go to Hell.* The traditionalist's view that death means eternal agony is so ingrained in our thinking, we *assume* verses like this communicate concepts to support our preconceived ideas.

3. Genesis 3:19: "By the sweat of your face you shall eat bread, till you return to the ground, for out of it you were taken; for you are dust, and to dust you shall return."

Note the clear teaching that humans are mortal. Conventional thinking has brought us the notion that we are all eternal. Hundreds of Scriptures clearly declare that *we are not eternal beings.* Eternal life is a gift, granted by God to those who have been given the gifts of repentance and faith in the finished work of Jesus Christ on the cross.

4. Psalm 21:9: "You will make them as a blazing oven when you appear. The Lord will swallow them up in His wrath, and fire will *consume them.*"

The Lord's fire is a "consuming fire." Fire does what it does: it destroys. Throughout Scripture we are told that the end of man is death. The idea of man's immortality may have originated in the writings of Aristotle and Socrates, and their influence carried into Hebrew culture approximately 350 years before Jesus's incarnation. Some claim that it may have formulated within various pagan religions as well.

5. Jude 7: ". . . just as Sodom and Gomorrah and the surrounding cities, which likewise indulged in sexual immorality and pursued unnatural desire, serve as an example by undergoing a punishment of *eternal fire.*"

The punishment that Sodom and Gomorrah experienced is not still burning; however, the eternal effect of that fire and destruction is still ongoing. What is the eternal punishment that awaits the lost? It is like that of Sodom and Gomorrah: utter destruction with eternal consequences. The wicked will *receive* an eternal punishment, not *endure* an eternal punishment.

6. Matthew 10:28: "And do not fear those who kill the body but cannot kill the soul. Rather fear Him who can destroy both soul and body in Hell."

The word "destroy" is used transitively, and its use in the synoptic gospels always means to kill or slay. Man can kill the body only. God can kill or slay the body and soul. The Greek word for "Hell" here is *Gehenna,* alluding to the place that used to be called *Topheth,* a "place of slaughter," where God's enemies were reduced to corpses which scavenging beasts would devour.

7. Mark 9:43, 47-48: "And if your hand causes you to sin, cut it off. It is better for you to enter life crippled than with two hands to go to

Hell, to the unquenchable fire . . . And if your eye causes you to sin, tear it out. It is better for you to enter the kingdom of God with one eye than with two eyes to be thrown into Hell, where their worm does not die and the fire is not quenched."

Jesus is quoting here from Isaiah 66:24, where God's fiery judgment resulted in piles of stinking, rotting, lifeless corpses. It is an assumption to believe that an "unquenchable" fire is an "eternal" fire. Unquenchable means that the fire cannot be stopped until it has done what fire does: it destroys. The worms will not stop until they have done what they do: fully consume. The fire at Sodom and Gomorrah was surely an unquenchable, eternal fire; however, as Jude 7 tells us, *its eternal fire is not still burning.* It "unquenchably" completed its task. Fire being referred to as eternal *may also mean that it is perfect and from Heaven,* unlike fire that man creates. Many times the fires that we start, such as the task of burning brush or logs, leave portions that are not reduced to ash. Man-made fires can sometimes be easily quenched or die out before everything is consumed. See Ezekiel 20:47.

The word "Hell" is used fifty-four times in some Bibles. It is translated from several different words with various meanings, as indicated below. The following terms are not synonymous with Hell. (A capital H is used in this book when referring to Heaven and Hell because they are proper names and real places, no different from the accepted practice when we write Hawaii or Hartford.)

In the Old Testament:

"Hell" is translated thirty-one times from the Hebrew *Sheol,* which means "the grave" or the dwelling place of the dead. (It might be noted that the traditional description of "Hell" does not occur in the OT.)

In the New Testament:

"Hell" is translated ten times from the Greek *Hades,* which means "the grave" or abode for those who have died, including Acts 2:31, where we see that Jesus was not to remain in the place of the dead or grave. Also, notice Psalm 16:10 as it uses *Sheol.*

"Hell" is translated twelve times from the Greek *Gehenna,* which means "a place of burning." (This word is used eleven times by Jesus and once by James.) Gehenna was a literal place: the smoldering dump outside Jerusalem, formerly a place of pagan child sacrifices.

"Hell" is translated one time from the Greek *Tartarus,* which means "a place of darkness." In some Greek literature this word did refer to a place of torment, but whatever it is, it is temporary, as seen in 2 Peter 2:4

NOTE: The word "Hell" is not in most Bibles that are *literal translations,* such as Young's Literal Translation Bible.

8. Ezekiel 18:21-22: "But if a wicked person turns away from all his sins [repents] and keeps all my statutes and does what is just and right, he shall surely live; he shall not die. None of the transgressions that he has committed shall be remembered against him; for the righteousness that he has done he shall live."

This chapter is full of contrasts between life and death. Never is there any indication of life with eternal and conscious agony. Verse 32 tells us too that God has "no pleasure in the death of anyone. So turn, and live." God never indicates or warns the house of Israel of any notion of eternal life for all with two options: one eternal life that is good and the other eternal life that is agonizing and painful. It is fail to repent and die, or repent and live.

9. John 3:36: "Whoever believes in the Son has eternal life; whoever does not obey the Son shall not see life, but the wrath of God remains on him."

Clearly, we can see the contrast here. Eternal life is set against the idea of not seeing life. If eternal agony is a reality, then those suffering it have to be alive. Jesus says quite openly that those who do not believe and choose to disobey will *not see life*. God's destructive wrath, as we've seen in Sodom and Gomorrah and Jude 7, will have its eternal effect on them.

What Does the Bible Tell Us About God's Punishment?

Throughout the Scripture we are told that God punishes with death—*not torture or prolonged agony*. If we want to have a proper understanding of final punishment for those who are not redeemed by Christ, we can look to hundreds of cases where the worst and ultimate punishment is death.

Nowhere do we see torture used on the lost or the wicked. Even if you subscribe to the idea (which is gaining attention recently) that Hell is not physical torture but some sort of mental anguish, brought on by a separation from God and an absence of any hope, you are still without biblical precedent. This hypothesis almost seems to be a concession by some traditionalists who have not accepted the overwhelming weight of Scripture which supports the conditionalist view, yet correspondingly can't give credence to the traditional view of physical, conscious agony for those who have not been redeemed by Christ.

Those hundreds of millions punished in Noah's day were destroyed—*quickly*. The thousands living in Sodom and Gomorrah were not put through some prolonged agony. They were destroyed *quickly* by what the Bible itself calls "eternal fire" that rained down from Heaven. And those eternal flames had an eternal effect on the inhabitants of those two cities, as we read in Jude 7.

Reading torture, or everlasting conscious torment, into the Bible is wrong, and those who do this should take their time to study this subject much more before they risk defaming the name of their God. To declare that God gives eternal life to the lost so that He can torment and torture them without end is a horrible thing—*because it's not true.* As Christians, we need to deliberate and reconsider the overwhelming biblical evidence to the contrary.

10. Malachi 4:1-3: "For behold, the day is coming, burning like an oven, when all the arrogant and all evildoers will be stubble. The day that is coming shall set them ablaze, says the LORD of hosts, so that it will leave them neither root nor branch. But, for you who fear my name, the sun of righteousness shall rise with healing in its wings. You shall go out leaping like calves from the stall. And you shall tread down the wicked, for they will be ashes under the soles of your feet, on the day when I act, says the LORD of hosts."

Here, the result of God's wrath, through the blaze of His destruction, is ashes—all that remains of those who have perished. This is not a picture of human souls in conscious torment.

11. Matthew 3:12: "His winnowing fork is in His hand, and He will clear His threshing floor and gather His wheat into the barn, but the chaff He will burn with unquenchable fire."

12. John 15:6: "If anyone does not abide in Me he is thrown away like a branch and withers; and the branches are gathered, thrown into the fire, and burned."

13. Matthew 13:30: "Let both [the weeds and the wheat] grow together until the harvest, and at harvest time I will tell the reapers,

'Gather the weeds first and bind them in bundles to be burned, but gather the wheat into my barn.'"

Jesus and John the Baptist compare the destiny of the lost to branches, chaff, and weeds that are thoroughly and unquestionably destroyed—with an effective and unquenchable fire. They are not set aside for an agonizing existence, but destruction. Most English Bible versions record this as an "unquenchable" fire. This does not mean eternal fire; it means that it *cannot be extinguished until it completes its destruction.* The International Standard Version uses the term "inextinguishable."

14. Revelation 14:11: Speaking of those who worship the beast, "And the smoke of their torment goes up forever and ever, and they have no rest, day or night, these worshipers of the beast and its image, and whoever receives the mark of its name."

The smoke of torment rising forever is an allusion to Isaiah 34:8-10's smoke rising forever from the destruction of Edom. Revelation 20 depicts the *abstract entities* of death and Hades thrown into the lake of fire, entities which could not be thrown into a lake of fire, let alone tormented. The truth that is being communicated here is *their utter end.* The imagery of torment, as made clear from Revelation 14, 18, and 19 and the allusion to Isaiah 34, is symbolism communicating destruction.

15. Revelation 20:14-15: "Then Death and Hades were thrown into the lake of fire. This is the second death, the lake of fire. And if anyone's name was not found written in the book of life, he was thrown into the lake of fire."

Hades is a description used in Scripture to designate a place of the dead. Gehenna was a literal place that was thought to contain a perpetually burning fire at the time of Jesus. It was the trash dump west of Jerusalem. Many English Bibles translate *Gehenna* as Hell, and it signifies a place of destruction. See Matthew 10:28.

16. Psalm 92:7: "When the wicked spring up like grass, and when all the workers of iniquity flourish, they are doomed to be *destroyed forever.*"

This again states that the lost will be doomed to destruction—forever. Just as a murderer who is given a lethal injection on death row is killed—forever. The weight of Scripture shows that the wicked will suffer eternal punishment, but not that they will have punishment actively inflicted on them for eternity. Punishment is a noun, not a verb. Punishment is the result of the verb *punish*. Thus, God punishes the person, and the result, the punishment, is everlasting. Likewise, the murderer executed on death row is eternally punished. His punishment is irreversible.

17. 1 Timothy 6:15–16: "Which He will display at the proper time—He who is the blessed and only Sovereign, the King of kings and Lord of lords, who *alone* has immortality, who dwells in unapproachable light, whom no one has ever seen or can see. To Him be honor and eternal dominion. Amen."

God alone has immortality. Traditionalists have promoted the notion that humans are immortal, and therefore, those who do not go to Heaven must exist somewhere—thus, Hell must be eternal. Immortality for people is a gift from God! *It is conditional.* See John 3:16.

18. Genesis 2:17: "But of the tree of the knowledge of good and evil you shall not eat, for in the day that you eat of it you shall surely die."

The sin of disobedience brought the curse, which included death—not only Adam and Eve's death, but the death of all their offspring. The Hebrew form of "die" used here is related to the idea of a *"death sentence" or pronouncement of death.* The expression "surely die" is from the Hebrew words *muth temuth* which is parallel to a death sentence. Also seen in Numbers 15:35.

After Adam and Eve sinned and were banned from the garden, God killed an animal. This very first shedding of blood, in which He made garments of skin and clothed them, was an act performed by God. It was not a cooperative act between man and God, but a gift from God. He did it all.

This act was prophetic of the redemption provided to us by Jesus's shedding of His blood. God does it all. Again, it is not a cooperative act between man and God, but a gift from God. He does it all.

Immediately after we read of the animal that God uses in Genesis 3:21, we see one of the most overlooked anomalies in all of the Bible. This curious, yet *profound* oddity exists at the end of verse 22.

Most translations, as well as Young's Literal Translation, read very much like the ESV: "The LORD God said, 'Behold, the man has become like one of Us in knowing good and evil. Now, lest he reach out his hand and take also of the tree of life and eat, and live forever—'"

Notice that this is an incomplete sentence. This is quite profound and penetrating if we take a closer look. This dash is known as an *aposiopesis,* and it is a clear indication of unspeakable omission.

There are two trees. The first we read about is the tree of the knowledge of good and evil, from which they did eat. The second tree is the tree of life.

What would have happened if Adam and Eve had been able to eat of this tree?

The very concept becomes unspeakable.

We know that they would live forever, but it is clear that *the idea of sinful man living forever is so dreadful and appalling that it is not even uttered.*

Man's default setting after he sinned is death. This verse clearly states that our destiny is death—not to live forever.

> The only condition by which we can have eternal life is adoption: to be removed from Adam's lineage and placed into the lineage of Jesus, the second Adam. And this is accomplished by God. He chooses and adopts us—it's not of ourselves. He does it all, and He deserves all the glory. (Read chapters 5 and 6 of Paul's Letter to the Romans for a fuller development of this.)

19. Psalm 103:9: "He will not always accuse, nor will He harbor His anger forever."

An eternal agony maintained by God on all the lost would represent the opposite of this passage and many others like it. See Psalm 30:5, Isaiah 57:16, Jeremiah 3:5 and 12, Micah 7:18, and 1 John 4:8 and 16.

20. Matthew 7:13–14: "Enter by the narrow gate. For the gate is wide and the way is easy that leads to *destruction,* and those who enter by it are many. For the gate is narrow and the way is hard that leads to *life,* and those who find it are few."

Contrast and clarity. *Destruction,* not torment or agony. This destruction is the antithesis to life.

21. Obadiah 1:16: "Because just as you drank on My holy mountain, all the nations will drink continually. They will drink and swallow and become as if they had never existed."

"To become as if they had never existed." Clearly gone. Out of existence.

22. Romans 4:17: "As it is written: 'I have made you a father of many nations.' He is our father in the sight of God, in whom he believed—the God who gives life to the dead and calls things that are not, as though they were."

In this chapter Paul is spelling out definitively the idea of life being acquired through faith. The lost are dead. The *pagan notion* that everyone is immortal is foreign and absent in Paul's writings.

23. Romans 6:13: "Do not present your members to sin as instruments for unrighteousness, but present yourselves to God as those who have been brought from death to life, and your members to God as instruments for righteousness."

Again, we see that death is the default setting. Life is the contrast, which is eternal life granted by God—a gift to those who were once heading for destruction.

24. James 5:20: "Remember this: Whoever turns a sinner from the error of his way will save his soul from death and cover over a multitude of sins."

Both the saved sinners and the lost sinners will die. The lost will suffer a second death, and this passage is addressing the issue of that second death. Saved sinners will be granted eternal life, avoiding the death James is describing. Note too that the soul suffers death. *The soul is not immortal* as many Christians think. Note Jesus's words in Matthew 10:28. "Stop being afraid of those who kill the body but can't kill the soul. Instead, be afraid of the one who can destroy both body and soul in Hell."

25. Matthew 13:39-42: "Just as the weeds are gathered and burned with fire, so will it be at the close of the age. The Son of Man will send His angels, and they will gather out of His kingdom all causes of sin and all law-breakers, and throw them into the fiery furnace. In that place there will be weeping and gnashing of teeth."

Just as weeds are burn*ed,* not continually burn*ing,* so too will the condemned be destroyed by fire. It is a consuming fire. The *gnashing of teeth* tells us that they will go *into* the fire with defiance and cursing, with no sign of repentance. For some reason, many Christians have been led to think that the gnashing of teeth indicates pain, which is not correct. Notice Acts 7:54.

26. Proverbs 11:19: "The truly righteous man attains life, but he who pursues evil goes to his death."

Everyone experiences the first death, but the one who pursues evil experiences the second death—while the righteous attain life.

27. Hebrews 6:8: "But land that produces thorns and thistles is worthless and is in danger of being cursed. In the end it will be burned."

The writer here is comparing thorns and thistles to those who lack true repentance. Their destiny is to be burned—*consumed* by fire. See 2 Samuel 23:7 and Isaiah 27:4.

28. James 1:15: "Then desire when it has conceived gives birth to sin, and sin when it is fully grown brings forth *death."*

29. Romans 5:12: "Therefore, just as sin entered the world through one man, and death through sin, and in this way *death* came to all men because all sinned."

30. Romans 8:13: "For if you are living the flesh, you are going to *die,* and if you are putting to death the practices of the body, you shall live."

31. Romans 6:21: "What benefit did you reap at that time from the things you are now ashamed of? Those things result in *death!"*

Notice that Paul never suggests, implies, or alludes to any sort of ongoing agony or conscious torment.

32. Psalm 37:1-2: "Do not fret because of evil men or be envious of those who do wrong; for like grass they will soon wither, like green plants they will soon *die away."*

33. Psalm 37:20: "But the wicked will *perish;* the enemies of the LORD are like the glory of the pastures; they vanish—like *smoke* they *vanish away."*

34. Psalm 37:38: "Sinners will come to an *end* together, and the *end* of the wicked is for *destruction."*

It's interesting that this passage says "together" they will come to an end. When Hades is thrown into the lake of fire, a final destruction will take place with all the condemned together. Also, they will vanish—like smoke. No better depiction exists to explain that something is *gone* than the image of smoke.

35. Matthew 8:12: "But many Israelites—those for whom the kingdom was prepared—will be thrown into outer darkness, where there will be weeping and gnashing of teeth."

This passage is clearly about those who thought they deserved a place of hierarchy in Heaven. Again, the gnashing of teeth is a term of defiance, not pain, as many have been led to believe.

36. Psalm 112:10: "The wicked man will see and be vexed, he will gnash his teeth and waste away; the longings of the wicked will come to *nothing.*"

Many of the psalms tell us clearly about the *destruction* of the lost. Imagine the day of judgment and the lost seeing Hell. Psalm 112:10 prophetically describes that day. The lost will be angry, thus the gnashing of teeth, when they see what's coming, and then will be destroyed—perish and waste away to nothing.

37. 1 John 5:11-13: "And the testimony is this, that God has given us eternal life, and this life is in His Son. He who has the Son has life; he who does not have the Son of God *does not have life.* These things I have written to you who believe in the name of the Son of God, so that you may know that you have eternal life."

The contrast is between eternal life or no life. Eternal life in Hell is life; despite its horror, the concept of eternal conscious agony is still life. This passage says those who do not have the Son are *without life.* Another clear contrast. It is a contradiction to Scripture to say that life will continue for the lost—even if it's in torment. That *is* life regardless of the idea that it would be a horrible life. *A torture-filled life is not the same thing as destruction.*

38. 2 Timothy 1:10: "But it has now been revealed through the appearing of our Savior, Christ Jesus, who has destroyed death and has brought life and immortality to light through the gospel."

Interestingly, "life and immortality" are correlated here—contrasted against the destruction of death.

39. Matthew 24:50-51: "The master will return unannounced and unexpected, and he will cut the servant to pieces and assign him a place with the hypocrites."

In this parable, we are introduced to a rare aspect of the destruction of the lost—the sword. Yet the picture is still death, perishing, and an end.

Taking a Closer Look at the Words
Forever, Everlasting, and *Eternal*

The words *forever* and *everlasting* have some interesting meanings in Scripture that are not necessarily what we assume. *They do not necessarily mean never-ending or eternal.* The Hebrew word *olam,* the Greek word *aion* (or eon), and even the Latin word *saeculum* can be interpreted as an undetermined period, or when referring to a much longer time, "aiones of aiones" or "saecula of saecula."

Jonah 2:6 reads, "At the roots of the mountains, I went down to the land whose bars closed upon me *forever;* yet You brought my life up from the pit, O Lord my God." This is part of Jonah's description regarding his time in the belly of the large fish. "Forever" in this situation was three days.

In 1 Samuel 1:22, 28 we are told, "But Hannah did not go up, for she said to her husband, 'As soon as the child is weaned, I will bring him, so that he may appear in the presence of the Lord and dwell there *forever."* This is from the narrative describing Samuel's birth and his mother's commitment to dedicate her new baby to full-time service at the house of the Lord and to the priest Eli. In this passage, "forever" undoubtedly means a lifetime.

Fire came down from Heaven at the consecration of
Solomon's temple. God said He would dwell there "forever,"
yet we know the temple was destroyed
and the fire put out. See Ezekiel 43:7 and 37:26.

In Deuteronomy 15:17 God commanded, "It shall come
about if he says to you, 'I will not go out from you,' because
he loves you and your household, since he fares well with
you; then you shall take an awl and pierce it through his ear
into the door, and he shall be your servant *forever.* Also you
shall do likewise to your maidservant." Again, this "forever"
is limited to a lifetime. This limited use of "forever" is found
throughout the Bible: 1 Samuel 27:12: "So Achish believed
David, saying, 'He has surely made himself odious among his
people Israel; therefore he will become my servant *forever.'*"
Philemon 1:15: "For this perhaps is why he was parted from
you for a while, that you might have him back *forever.*" This is
Paul's writing to Philemon regarding the return of Onesimus.
Forever in this case could be months, years, or decades—or for
the rest of his life. Consider Exodus 21:6 and Deuteronomy
15:17, where we are told that the slave will have his ear pierced
and be his master's servant forever. *"Forever" is clearly relative
here.* Deuteronomy 23:3 seems to equivocate forever with ten
generations in this particular situation, and 1 Samuel 27:12
limits forever to the period of time that Samuel stayed with Eli.

Exodus 12:24: "You shall observe this rite as a statute for
you and for your sons forever." The Passover was to be kept
forever. However, it ended in the New Testament: Hebrews
9:24-26. Exodus 40:15: "For their anointing shall surely be
an everlasting priesthood throughout their generations." This
"everlasting priesthood" also ended in the New Testament
period: Hebrews 7:11-14.

Liddell and Scott's Greek Lexicon, considered for many years to be one of the great concordances, states under the word "eternal": "The words eternal, everlasting, forever, are *sometimes* taken for a long time, and are *not always* to be understood strictly."

The term "for ever" or "forever," meaning a period of time, limited or unlimited, is used fifty-six times in the Bible in connection with things that have already ended.

40. Revelation 20:10: "And the devil who had deceived them was thrown into the lake of fire and sulfur where the beast and the false prophet were, and they will be tormented day and night forever and ever."

When considering the general acceptance of the traditional view of Hell as eternal torture or torment, it is important to understand these two *presumptions* collide when we read Revelation 20:10.

A) It is assumed that "forever" means eternal, with no end.

B) It is assumed that people are immortal.

If we understand that the Bible does not teach the immortality of man, we can see that *only those who have been given the gift of eternal life through Jesus will experience immortality.* As we consider the common understanding of the biblical term "forever," the verse means something different from the assumed traditionalist view.

The "everlasting" torment of Revelation 20:10 describes the devil. Verses 6 and 14 tell us of the second death. If we are to assume that verse 10 is describing an endless existence in torment, then all the Scripture that clearly describes destruction must be wrong, and the second death described in verses 6 and 14 must be wrong—unless we somehow presume that the lost are *again brought back after the second death* to experience a life of endless torment.

41. Matthew 25:41: "Then shall He say also unto them on the left hand, depart from me ye cursed, into everlasting fire, prepared for the devil and his angels." (KJV)

This and Revelation 20:10 are considered the strongest verses in favor of the traditionalist's view of Hell. Considering the many scriptural passages telling us that man is mortal and the fact that *forever* and *everlasting* do not always mean without end, *these verses are in concert (not disagreement)* with the many passages of Scripture telling us that the *end of man is destruction* unless he is redeemed by God through the finished work of His Son.

If the Bible uses the word *eternal* to describe an event that took hours and *forever* to describe periods of time such as three days or a few decades—

Can We Know How "Eternal" and "Forever" Should Be Understood?

Consider this statement that describes the biblical languages:

The descriptive adjective does not determine the age. The subject determines the age. This is important to understand when we're examining this issue. The subject determines the age, not the adjective.

Consider the fact that the Bible uses terms like *eternal* and *forever* to describe events that lasted various periods of time from hours, days, decades, and unending time. So how are we to understand passages which defy our understanding and seem to be somewhat contradictory?

If eternal doesn't mean eternal, then we seem to have a difficulty. In modern vernacular: "Houston. We have a problem."

If you're not sure about this, then consider these notes from Podcast 14 on www.rethinkinghell.com. The host, Chris Date, and his guest, Dr. Robert Allen Taylor, discuss the book, *Rescue From Death: John 3:16 Salvation.*

* The "Eternal Punishment" Jesus speaks of in Matthew 25:46 does not tell us what the punishment is.
* Traditionalists have forged the idea into our culture, without proper exegesis, that "eternal punishment" must mean suffering. In their thinking, this is apparently the only form of punishment possible here.
* Most all "punishment" in Scripture is clearly stated as death. *Not suffering or agony.*
* Interestingly, the contrast or parallel to eternal life is "eternal death." Not "eternal suffering." Suffering is not inherently or instinctually logical, *nor biblically shown.*
* "Eternal" describes nouns of action, like eternal redemption and eternal salvation as we see in Hebrews. Eternal can describe the duration of the outcome of the verb, rather than its process. We are eternally redeemed, but God is not *eternally "redeeming"* us. Yet our redemption is unendingly eternal.
* In Greek, it is the noun that determines how long an age will last. (Greek: *aeonius* or *aeon.*)
* Consider the "age of a man," or the "age of a tree," or the "age of a mountain." The age actually comes from the noun—not the adjective "age." The same adjective is used each time, but we know that the age of a tree and the age of a mountain are not the same.
* The adjective "age" or aeonius does not make its subject eternal.
* It's the noun or subject that determines the duration of aeonius, or age.
  [Consider how we use the word "love" in English. "I love pie," "I love to ride my motorcycle," or "I love my wife"—the subject determines the meaning or intensity of "love." I don't love pie the same way I love my wife. This is similar to the way the words "eternal" and "forever" are used in Scripture.]

* We, as believers, have eternal life in Christ. Not because eternal life is inherent—because it is not. It's also not because the word "eternal" is used to describe our salvation.

* The reason redeemed believers have become immortal and will experience endless, without end, life eternal is this: We are joined to the ONE who is eternal. Jesus will never die and will always exist. *He has linked us with Himself.* This is a beautiful and miraculous act of His mercy and grace—He has adopted us!

* Jesus, the subject or noun, determines our eternal nature. Not the word "eternal."

* Marvin R. Vincent (1834-1922) the author of *Word Studies in the New Testament,* first published in 1887 in four volumes, summarizes this well: "The life and unity with Christ is endless. This fact is not expressed by aeonius."

* It is *not the adjective that imparts* eternity into the life that believers have in Christ. It's the nature of the believers' *union with Christ* that allows us to understand the adjective to mean eternal.

* The "eternal fire" that destroyed Sodom and Gomorrah lasted as long as it was necessary for it to destroy, therefore, the adjective "eternal" acquires its real meaning from the thing it was linked to—a successful and destructive fire. It lasted as long as was needed to destroy.

* Our life is described as everlasting, never ending, eternal because the subject that we're linked to is Jesus—the creator and sustainer of the universe. This is profound and well worth our contemplation and reflection.

* Traditionalists say that there is a parallel between the life we have in Christ and the punishment. Well, if life is to be eternal—then we need a contrasting punishment that is eternal. Here's the critical question: "What punishment is inherently eternal?"

* Torment, pain, agony, suffering, etc.—none of these are inherently eternal.

* Punishment does not necessarily mean suffering and rarely means that in the Bible.

* Traditional views on eternal punishment have serious problems.

    *   Praise God—We, as redeemed and adopted children, are joined to Christ eternal—and our salvation acquires its unendingness from Jesus, as the subject (or noun) that is ETERNAL.

42. Job 12:10: "For the life of every living thing is in his hand, and the breath of every human being."

Evil and sin will be defeated, and the kingdom of God will be eternally triumphant. A belief in eternal life in Hell requires a) evil and sin to be eternal and b) God's hand to sustain the life of every person in Hell for an unending eternity. If the wicked are eternally separated from God and He is omnipresent, then the destruction of the lost is the only scriptural conclusion possible. They must be ended like smoke. *All life is sustained by God;* even Hitler's ability to breathe moment by moment was by God's hand. See Psalm 54:4, 3:5, 139, Jeremiah 38:16, Daniel 5:23.

43. Luke 16:19-31: The Parable of the Rich Man and Lazarus

This passage has been used as a teaching about Hell when it is not. In fact, the term used in this parable is Hades. Also, another familiar story dates back generations before it was incorporated into this parable. Jesus was addressing people who tended to consider wealth as a sign of God's blessing and poverty as a type of judgment on others.

The simple message of this parable falls in line with the other teachings in Luke. Jesus told it to highlight the truths that the first would be last and the last would be first, as well as the fact that they had Moses and the prophets—and hearing a message from someone who regretted his ways was *not* going to convince them.

Some important points about this story:

- This is a parable, not an allegory. A parable carries one central theme, and that theme seems apparent if we look to the parables surrounding it.
- There is no precedent or sound reason to consider it a true story simply because it contains a proper name, Lazarus.
- The central subject matches the primary issue Luke is showing us in this account. After some research and thought, it becomes

clear that this is not a discourse on Heaven and Hell. If it was a discourse on Heaven and Hell or salvation, then we would need to conclude that 1) the poor and/or downtrodden immediately go to Heaven and 2) the rich go to Hell.

- Abraham's bosom is not Heaven. Hebrews 11:8-16.
- The dead know nothing according to Ecclesiastes 9:5.
- If this was a treatise on Hell, then there is communication and an open view between Heaven and Hell.
- Rewards are given at Christ's second coming, *not at death.* Revelation 22:11-12.
- The lost are sent to Hell *after* judgment. Based on biblical chronology, the rich man can't be in Hell yet.
- Most Bibles translate this place as "Hell." However, the actual term in Greek is *Hades* because it is clearly not the place of final punishment. Hades is the interim place of the dead, so even if this were a true story (not a parable), it doesn't tell us what the result will be for the lost after final judgment.
- If the proper interpretation should be that the rich man is in flames, a drop of water on his tongue would be useless.
- This parable has been misused for centuries to promote the doctrine of an endless burning Hell and is a misuse of God's Word and a blatant misrepresentation of His character in light of the overwhelming weight of Scripture that declares the *destruction* of the lost and the fact that salvation comes from faith in the finished work of Christ—not from being poor.

The Jews of Jesus's day believed that riches were a sign of God's favor while poverty was the result of His displeasure. The rich man here represents the self-righteous Jews. They had access to God's Word, yet they treated the Gentiles like scum. *They were wasting the riches of God's revelation* as seen in the parable of the unjust steward a few verses earlier in Luke 16:1-13.

Lazarus represents the Gentiles, who were receiving nothing from the Jews. Jesus makes it clear with this parable that the Jews who placed themselves above the Gentiles would find themselves in *irreversible regret, while the poor man, Lazarus, would be comforted* and greeted by Abraham. The Jews had serious misunderstandings about who was saved and who was lost. One major point of this parable is that the first will be last and the last will be first, as we also see in Luke 13:30.

The name *Lazarus* here was perhaps also prophetic. A short time later Jesus would raise a young man named Lazarus from the dead. This catapulted the chief priests into a plot to kill Jesus and Lazarus (John 12:10).

Martin Luther, the great reformer, taught that this was a parable, not a true story—nor a revelation about the afterlife. He states, "Therefore we conclude that the bosom of Abraham signifies nothing else than the Word of God . . . the hell here mentioned cannot be the true hell that will be at the day of judgment. For the corpse of the rich man is without doubt not in hell, but buried in the earth; it must however be a place where the soul can be and has no peace, and it cannot be corporeal [punishment]."

44. Matthew 25:30: "And cast the worthless servant into the outer darkness. In that place there will be weeping and gnashing of teeth."

Similar to the parable of the rich man and Lazarus, the parable here is about regret and hardness of heart with the mention of "weeping" and "gnashing of teeth." Traditionalists have continued to use this verse to support the idea of torment lasting forever. Undoubtedly, the lost will be weeping and gnashing their teeth as they are thrown into the consuming fire of Hell. Psalm 112:10 says, "The wicked man sees it and is *angry; he gnashes* his teeth and *melts away;* the desire of the wicked will perish!"

45. Galatians 6:8: "For he that sows to his flesh, shall of the flesh reap corruption; but he that sows to the Spirit shall of the Spirit reap life everlasting."

One more contrast is seen here: *corruption* or *everlasting life.* The writer could have added "everlasting pain" or "everlasting torment"; however, the term he uses is "corruption." Acts 2:31 reads, "Seeing what was ahead, he spoke of the resurrection of the Christ, that he was not abandoned to the grave, nor did his body see *corruption.*" *Corruption means decay. Decay means to perish or degenerate.* Galatians 6:8 tells us that reliance on the flesh leads to corruption, decay, and perishing.

46. James 4:12: "The only real Lawgiver and Judge is He who is able to save or to destroy. Who are you to sit in judgment on your fellow man?"

God saves or destroys. If God wants us to think that we are immortal beings and that the lost will burn in Hell eternally, without end, then why is this language of *destroying, death, perishing, vanishing,* etc. used over and over?

There Are Many Areas of Agreement

Conditionalism is not an attack on the central elements of Christianity. The conditionalists' view about what happens at the Lake of Fire is actually the only area of departure from most traditionalists' views.
Our similarities are many.
If we were to make a list of orthodox doctrines that each of us hold, we would likely agree on 90 percent—the question that is at issue is this: Will the lost be destroyed after judgment *or* will the lost be *kept alive* to experience agony for eternity?

---

47. Ezekiel 18:4: "Behold, all souls are Mine; the soul of the father as well as the soul of the son is Mine. The soul who sins will die."

48. Matthew 25:46: "And these will go away into eternal punishment, but the righteous into eternal life."

Their punishment is eternal. No reversal. No coming back. It will last for eternity. Why should we assume this is suggesting that the lost will be enduring eternal conscious torture? *Eternal punish<u>ment</u>. Not eternal punish<u>ing</u>.*

ETERNAL PUNISHMENT is the opposite of eternal life,
not *another form of eternal life.*
It is explained by Paul as "the punishment of
eternal destruction" (2 Thessalonians 1:9),
and by Jude as a fate like that of Sodom and Gomorrah,
which was obliterated (Jude 7).
Are we to reason that the lost will be
destroyed over and over and over?

49. John 5:28-29: "Do not be amazed at this, for a time is coming when all who are in their graves will hear His voice and come out—those who have done good will rise to live, and those who have done evil will rise to be condemned."

This is another opportunity for the Scriptures to declare "eternal torment" or "everlasting fire." However, the Scriptures continue to use terms like *judgment, damnation,* and *condemnation* to describe what will happen to those who have avoided God's mercy.

50. Ezekiel 28:18: "By the multitude of your iniquities, in the unrighteousness of your trade you profaned your sanctuaries; so I brought fire out from your midst; it consumed you, and I turned you to ashes on the earth in the sight of all who saw you."

Why should we think God's fire does not consume? His Word makes it clear. Fire consumes and leaves ashes.

51. John 6:48-51: "I am the bread of life. Your forefathers ate the manna in the desert, yet they all died. This is the bread that comes down from Heaven, so that a person may eat it and not die. I am the living bread that came down from Heaven. If anyone eats this bread, he will live forever. And the bread I will give for the life of the world is my flesh."

Jesus uses the term "not die"—yet everyone dies. This passage tells us about the second death. After the first death there will be judgment, then either an everlasting death or life eternal. Note, too, that living eternally is exclusive to the saved. The traditionalists' view of *eternal life in Hell* is diametrically opposed to this passage.

52. Philippians 3:18-19: "For many, of whom I have often told you and now tell you even with tears, walk as enemies of the cross of Christ. Their end is destruction, their god is their belly, and they glory in their shame, with minds set on earthly things."

Beautifully, Paul tells us that he is broken over the lost, as indicated by his tears. He makes it clear that their end is destruction. Here is a golden opportunity for *clarity* about the destiny of the lost. *No indication is given by Paul that their end is endless conscious agony.*

53. 2 Peter 2:6: "If He condemned the cities of Sodom and Gomorrah by burning them to ashes, and made them an example of what is going to happen to the ungodly . . ."

"Ashes." This certainly doesn't sound like conscious agony. If you want an example of what will happen to the ungodly—here it is!

54. 2 Peter 2:12: "But these men blaspheme in matters they do not understand. They are like brute beasts, creatures of instinct, born only to be caught and destroyed, and like beasts they too will perish."

Can Paul make it any more clear? Again, he tells us that man's mortality is like an animal's—they will perish. Unless traditionalists find some basis for the endless torment of animals, then plainly the wicked will suffer death just as animals do.

55. John 11:25-26: "Jesus said to her, 'I am the resurrection and the life. Whoever believes in me, though he die, yet shall he live, and everyone who lives and believes in me shall never die. Do you believe this?'"

After all are resurrected for judgment, those who believe in Jesus will be given the gift of eternal life; horribly, all others will experience punishment and then final destruction. There is no indication that we will *all* live, with some to eternal life in Heaven and others to eternal life in Hell. Death is the clear teaching here. *It is the default setting for man.* See Genesis 3:22.

56. Hebrews 10:39: "But we are not of those who shrink back and are destroyed, but of those who believe and are saved."

Destruction is the opposite of being saved—not eternal *life* in fire or agony.

57. Psalm 49:20: "A man who has riches without understanding is like the beasts that perish."

Again, the lost are destroyed and perish just like animals. Man is not immortal without God's gift of eternal life.

58. 2 Thessalonians 1:7-9: "This will happen when the Lord Jesus is revealed from Heaven in blazing fire with His powerful angels. He will punish those who do not know God and do not obey the gospel of our Lord Jesus. They will be punished with everlasting destruction and shut out from the presence of the Lord and from the majesty of His power." (NIV)

The phrase "shut out" does not exist in the Greek text and only shows up in some of the popular translations. Some think that "shut out" indicates that a form of existence must be going on. In other words, you can't be shut out unless you are experiencing some semblance of existence. However, the lost will be irreversibly destroyed—unable to ever be in the presence of the Lord. God is omnipotent and omniscient, which would mean He is present even in Hell. Even in Hell, the lost would be in the presence of God. Destroyed means that they will not be in the presence of the Lord— they are eternally shut out!

59. 2 Peter 3:7: "By the same word the present heavens and earth are reserved for fire, being kept for the day of judgment and destruction of ungodly men."

After the second coming and the day of judgment, the lost will be destroyed. If the lost are to be sent to unending agony, *why do we keep reading about the destruction of the lost?* (This same description is used one verse earlier when Peter tells us what happened to the people during the flood.) This passage also tells us that the ungodly are probably not conscious in Hell now, but are *reserved* to experience their time in Hell after they are brought from their first death back to life for judgment. This is not to say that the saved are not with the Lord now, but the lost are likely in an unconscious state until judgment.

60. Psalm 146:4: "His breath departs, he returns to the earth; in that very day his thoughts perish."

If man is immortal, as the traditionalists say, how could a man's thoughts perish?

61. Psalm 1:6: "For the Lord knows the way of the righteous, but the way of the wicked will perish."

62. Psalm 68:2: "As *smoke is driven away,* so you shall drive them away; as *wax melts* before fire, so the wicked shall *perish* before God!"

63. Ecclesiastes 9:5: "For the living know that they will die, but *the dead know nothing;* they have no further reward, and even the memory of them is forgotten."

"The dead know nothing." This is the opposite of the traditionalist teaching of *conscious* torment.

64. 1 Corinthians 15:53–54: "For this perishable body must put on the imperishable, and this mortal body must put on immortality. When the perishable has been clothed with the imperishable, and the mortal with immortality, then the saying that is written will come true: Death has been swallowed up in victory."

Paul is explaining what will happen after the resurrection of the dead *for believers.* The default setting for man is mortality—which is described as *death, destruction, perishing, ashes, smoke, melting wax, unconsciousness, vanishing away,* etc. See verse 42—this is an explanation of what the redeemed can anticipate.

Grasping a Better Understanding of the End of Death and Resurrection

"For as by a man came death, by a man has come also the resurrection of the dead" (1 Corinthians 15:21). *Anastasis* is the Greek term used here for "resurrection," but it's the same word used when Jesus resurrected several people as recorded in the gospels, and it does not mean they received unending life at that point.

"For as in Adam all die, even so, in Christ shall all be made alive" (1 Corinthians 15:22). *Zoopoiethesontai* is the Greek term used here for "make alive." This is a future passive verb meaning "to enliven, animate beyond the reach of death."

There are actually three types of being "made alive":

1) Christ, the first fruit, is made alive. "First fruit" is singular in the Greek (the KJV incorrectly shows this to be plural). 1 Corinthians 15:23.
2) Those who are redeemed by Christ are made alive. 1 Thessalonians 4:13-18.
3) Those who are raised for the judgment are made alive. Revelation 20:13-15.

64. Hebrews 10:26-27: "If we deliberately keep on sinning after we have received the knowledge of the truth, no sacrifice of sins is left, but only a fearful expectation of judgment and of raging fire that will consume the enemies of God."

Again, we are told that *fire consumes*. Why doesn't Paul warn of a fire that "torments," "tortures," or "holds eternally in conscious agony"? This is another opportunity to give clear warning, yet the *overwhelming weight of Scripture* warns us of destruction. Why must traditionalists latch on to this belief that destruction is not bad enough? It is terribly horrendous. To be eternally taken out of the presence of God by destruction through Hell's fire—that's dreadful. But to avoid these passages—*once they have become aware of these Scriptures*—and continue to tell others that Hell is conscious torture without end *when there is so much biblical evidence to the contrary* is a needless mischaracterization of our Creator, Savior, and Sustainer.

65. Isaiah 66:24: "And they shall go out and look on the dead bodies of the men who have rebelled against me. For their worm shall not die, their fire shall not be quenched, and they shall be an abhorrence to all flesh."

This verse is quoted by Jesus in Mark 9. Only the second half of this verse is usually quoted by traditionalists. Again, context is critical. Read all of chapter 66. If you do, verse 24b cannot be used the improper way it has been used by those promoting eternal torture of the lost. It is preceded by terms like "dead bodies," "slain by the Lord," and "shall come to an end." See the notes above for number 7, Mark 9:48.

66. 1 Corinthians 15:26: "The last enemy to be destroyed is death."

Some traditionalists hold to the concept that there is some sort of "eternal death," as though Hell is an eternal and endless process of death. It is clear from this verse that death will also be destroyed. See also Revelation 20:14.

67. Nahum 1:8-10: "But with overflowing flood He will make a complete end of its site, and will pursue His enemies into darkness. Whatever you devise against the Lord, He will make a complete end of it. Distress will not rise up twice. Like tangled thorns, and like those who are drunken with their drink, they are consumed as stubble completely withered."

When the Lord destroys, He makes a *complete end* of it. His enemies will be *destroyed as stubble.* Lifeless.

68. Isaiah 13:9: "Behold, the day of the Lord is coming, cruel, with fury and burning anger, to make the land a desolation; and He will *exterminate* its sinners from it."

69. Isaiah 47:14: "Behold, they shall be as stubble; the fire shall burn them; they shall not deliver themselves from the power of the flame; there shall not be a coal to warm at, nor a fire to sit before."

This description of fire is of Babylon. If we are to use Scripture to interpret Scripture—even though this description is historical—it is clear *again* that fire destroys. Then it leaves *no warmth when it is complete.* The eternal fires of Sodom and Gomorrah and Edom left no coals to warm by today. Hell will "burn them up," and *no heat will ever come forth again.*

70. Isaiah 65:17: "For behold, I create new heavens and a new earth, and the former things shall not be remembered or come into mind."

Hell will have completed its gruesome job of destroying the lost. Just as the coals of Babylon, Gomorrah, and Edom have cooled and all things are new—*the fire of Hell will lead to Paradise restored!*

71. Revelation 21:4: "He will wipe every tear from their eyes. There will be no more death or mourning or crying or pain, for the old order of things has passed away."

Clearly, the new order of things will be in place. Paradise is restored. No more crying. No more pain. How could the lost be experiencing pain and torment? We read clearly here that there will be no more pain! Praise God! Hell is gone!

Why Do Traditionalists Hold This View?

1) For the most part, they have not seen the evidence. Every traditionalist I've encountered misrepresents or misunderstands the view presented here when they defend their position.

2) Some are steadfast in their position, and *no evidence* will change them.

3) Others refuse to study the Bible's evidence for this view because they think conditionalism is:

A) A view held by people who just can't cope with the traditional idea of eternal agony and torment of the lost.

B) A liberal view that will lead to a slippery slope of faulty theology.

C) A doctrine held by groups such as the Jehovah's Witnesses and Seventh-day Adventists and therefore wrong.

D) The opposite of what they have learned to be biblical truth that can't be questioned. A radical departure or heresy. They have heard sermons all their lives and seen the passages that seem to prove that Hell is eternal, unending agony for the lost. Therefore, they have closed their minds.

E) Too complicated. A subject that should be left to the professional theologians and pastors.

Many pastors and seminarians are in fear of social pressure and loss of tenure. One prominent university president who publicly declared his conversion from the traditionalist view stated that many of his colleagues could not "come out of this closet" for these reasons. A prominent pastor of a large denomination was fired six months before retiring and had his retirement income stripped after he publicly embraced conditionalism.

Every traditionalist I've heard in debates, sermons, or podcasts, as well as in their articles and books, misleads their audience (whether intentionally or not) regarding the actual views held by conditionalists. As fellow believers, this is perplexing.

Where Did Endless Torment Originate?

Samuel G. Dawson gives a thorough and lengthy explanation of the origin of "endless torment" doctrine in his book, *The Teaching of Jesus*. These three paragraphs are from chapter 11, "Jesus' Teaching on Hell." These give us a brief sense of how this biblically unsound notion began.

As we've seen, it most certainly did not originate in the Old Testament, either before or during the Mosaic Law. A great deal of evidence (more than we'll give here) suggests that it originated in Egypt, and the concept was widespread in the religious world. Augustine, commenting on the purpose of such doctrines, said:

"This seems to have been done on no other account, but as it was the business of princes, out of their wisdom and civil prudence, to deceive the people in their religion; princes, under the name of religion, persuaded the people to believe those things true, which they themselves knew to be idle fables; by this means, for their own ease in government, tying them the more closely to civil society." (Augustine, *City of God,* Book IV, p. 32, cited by Thayer, *Origin & History,* p. 37.)

Contriving doctrines to control people? Who would have believed it? Well, the Greek world did, the Roman world did, and evidently between the testaments, the Jews got involved, as well, as the concept of endless torment began appearing in the apocryphal books written by Egyptian Jews.

Are Sin and Evil Eternal?

There is an end to evil. It is clear in Revelation 21:5 that all things are going to be made new. "And he who was seated on the throne said, 'Behold, I am making all things new.' Also he said, 'Write this down, for these words are trustworthy and true.'" Unless we should assume that sin and evil will be reintroduced, then evil must be destroyed.

What could be more evil than billions of conscious, living sinners cursing God and gnashing their teeth forever and ever—unendingly? Are we to suppose that this evil will be sustained beyond the day that God makes *all* things new?

Three verses later we read, "But as for the cowardly, the faithless, the detestable, as for murderers, the sexually immoral, sorcerers, idolaters, and all liars, their portion will be in the lake that burns with fire and sulfur, which is the second death."

The second death. This involves clear language of total destruction. The end of the wicked will be just like Sodom and Gomorrah.

Who can stand before His indignation?
Who can endure the heat of His anger?
His wrath is poured out like fire,
and the rocks are broken into pieces by Him.
The LORD is good,
a stronghold in the day of trouble;
He knows those who take refuge in Him.
But with an overflowing flood
He will make a *complete end* of the adversaries,
and will pursue His enemies into darkness.
What do you plot against the LORD?
He will make a complete end;
trouble will not rise up a second time.
For they are like entangled thorns,
like drunkards as they drink;
they are *consumed* like dried stubble in fire.
Nahum 1:6-10

Revelation 21:4 sounds the final note: "He will wipe away every tear from their eyes, and *death shall be no more, neither shall there be mourning, nor crying, nor pain anymore, for the former things have passed away.*"

Quotes *Not* Worth Requoting

This is a small sampling of the many quotes by traditionalists on the subject of Hell. Some of these are very disturbing, especially in consideration that these were written by Christian leaders and writers. After reading the Scriptures above, it is obvious that *these people have relied on a very shallow and superficial understanding of what the Bible says about Hell.* It's very sad that so many have been taught these ideas over the centuries. *If we would only remove ourselves from the influence of men's ideas and hold to the clear teaching of God's Word!*

These quotes are further proof that very *bright and loving people will follow presuppositional ideas developed by their culture* and fail to establish for themselves the straightforward reading of Scripture.

"What bliss will fill the ransomed souls,
When they in glory dwell,
To see the sinner as he rolls,
In quenchless flames of hell."—from a hymn by Isaac Watts

". . . vast waves and billows of fire continually rolling over their heads, of which they shall forever be full of a quick sense within and without; their heads, their eyes, their tongues, their hands, their feet, their loins and *their vitals, shall forever be full of a flowing, melting fire,* fierce enough to melt the very rocks and elements; and also, they shall eternally be *full of the most quick and lively sense to feel the torments;* not for one minute, not for one day, not for one age, not for two ages, not for a hundred ages, nor for ten thousand millions of ages, one after another, but forever and ever, without any end at all, and never to be delivered."—Jonathan Edwards

"Husbands shall see their wives, parents shall see their children tormented before their eyes . . . the bodies of the damned shall be crowded together in hell like grapes in a wine-press, which press on another till they burst . . . assailed with its own appropriate and most *exquisite sufferings."*—Jeremy Taylor, the Church of England

"Therefore the saved shall go forth . . . to see the torments of the lost, seeing which they will not be grieved, but will be *satiated with joy* at the sight of the unutterable calamity of the lost."—Peter Lombard

"Constantly the damned will be judged, constantly they will suffer pain, and constantly they will be a fiery oven, that is, they will be *tortured* within by supreme distress and tribulation."—Martin Luther. When questioned whether the Blessed will not be saddened by seeing their nearest and dearest tortured, he answered, "Not in the least."

". . . the fire of divine wrath which *tortures* them is never quenched, and the worm of conscience which gnaws them never dies . . ."—John Gill

". . . the Blessed will see their friends and relations among the damned as often as they like but *without the least of compassion.*"—Johann Gerhard

"Which sight gives me joy? As I see illustrious monarchs groaning in the lowest darkness, philosophers as fire consumes them! . . . What inquisitor or priest in his munificence will bestow on you the favor of seeing and *exulting* in such things as these?"—Tertullian of Carthage (AD 160-240). Perhaps the earliest writer to promote a mixture of early Christian teachings with the Greek philosophy of immortality.

"In order that the happiness of the saints may be more delightful to them and that they may render more copious *thanks to God for it, they are allowed to see* perfectly the sufferings of the damned."—Thomas Aquinas.

Many of these quotes imply believers will
experience joy and satisfaction
in seeing the lost <u>surviving torture for unending eternity</u>.
*It's hard to believe anyone who calls themselves a Christian
can ever agree with such horror—
especially when we now see that the Scriptures teach differently.*

"The view of the misery of the damned will double the intensity of the love and gratitude of the saints of heaven."—Jonathan Edwards

"Souls with their bodies will be reserved in infinite *tortures* for suffering."—Cyprian of Carthage

"You will not surely die."—the Serpent to the woman, Genesis 3:4.

The first lie was this one. Satan was the first to preach the *immortality of man*. God warned Adam that he would *die* if he ate of the tree. Then Satan told Eve the very opposite. Traditionalists have popularized this same lie, that man is immortal by nature. The early church allowed this belief to pervade its teachings around AD 300. If the church held to the notion that man is immortal, and all are not saved, then the only conclusion is that the lost must experience endless eternity somewhere, thus, an eternal Hell must exist. Here we are today still dealing with the very first lie: "You will not surely die."

Quotes Worth Requoting

"I have no criticism of 'the doctrine of eternal punishment.' I teach the doctrine of eternal punishment. What I criticize (and totally reject) is the interpretation of 'eternal punishment' which says *that God will make the wicked immortal in order to torment them forever and ever without end.*

"The Bible does teach 'ongoing punishment' following the Judgment. That is the punishment of everlasting destruction, the second death. The person who suffers this fate will truly 'die,' 'perish' and be 'destroyed'—forever and ever without end. That destiny—not eternal conscious torment—*is the 'eternal punishment' of which Jesus solemnly warned."*—Edward Fudge

With regards to the way traditionalists use the book of Revelation: "But suddenly when it comes to defending the doctrine of the eternal torments of the damned in hell, the *symbolic nature* of much of the language in the book of Revelation disappears. Now all of a sudden, but only when defending their doctrine of hell (as eternal conscious agony). It stands out, that for people who are not known for their bizarre literalism in general, when it comes to the book of Revelation. You *suddenly become literalists* when the doctrine of hell is in question. A sudden change in rules when it suits your position."—Dr. Glenn Peoples

"How can you be perishing for eternity? Either you perish or you don't perish."—C.S. Lewis

Regarding the *responsibility* many respected traditionalists hold: "Sometimes when a scholar in your position says something, your readers or listeners will follow your leading because they don't know Greek and Hebrew . . . As Peter Parker's uncle told him in the movie *Spiderman,* 'With great power comes great responsibility.' You shouldn't employ, or allow others in your camp, to get away with persuading people with techniques that you wouldn't let one of your students get away with in another subject area."—Dr. Glenn Peoples

"I am convinced that most people, including most practicing Christians, are muddled and misguided on this topic [of the afterlife] and that this muddle produces quite serious mistakes in our thinking, our praying, our liturgies, our practice, and perhaps particularly our mission to the world."—N.T. Wright

Well-respected theologian D.A. Carson warns people about what he calls an "exegetical fallacy." The fallacy involves the "unwarranted adoption of an expanded semantic field. It lies in the assumption that the meaning of a word in a specific context is much broader than the context itself allows and may bring with it the word's entire semantic range. This step is sometimes called illegitimate totality transfer."

"This issue has been more widely discussed among Evangelical Christians than ever before and the view [Edward] Fudge advocates is undoubtedly now favored by more Evangelical Christians than ever before."—Richard Bauckham, Cambridge, England, 2011

"I feel that the time has come when I must declare my mind honestly. I believe that endless torment is a hideous and unscriptural doctrine which has been a terrible burden on the mind of the church for many centuries and a terrible blot on her presentation of the gospel. I should indeed be happy if, before I die, I could help in sweeping it away. Most of all I should *rejoice to see a number of theologians . . . joining . . . in researching this great topic with all its ramifications."*—John Wenham, well-known scholar and author of *The Elements of New Testament Greek,* which has been a standard textbook for decades.

The following is a candid response of one employee of an evangelical publisher, when asked what she thought of a book featuring a debate between traditionalism and conditionalism: "I certainly hope that annihilationism [conditionalism] is true! *It is not our place to hope that certain things are true* with reference to the things of God. It is our place to humbly receive the Word that God has given. That means restraining our curiosity where the Word is silent. And that means believing and obeying God's truth even if we don't like it."

"Christians have professed appalling theologies which made God into a sadistic monster . . . Hell is not eternal torment, but it is the final and irrevocable choosing of that which is opposed to God so completely and so absolutely that the only end is total non-being."—The Church of England's Doctrine Commission, February 1995. While some have claimed emotionalism to be the basis for the Church of England's change on this issue, we can see now that their position is clearly and unmistakably based on Scripture.

"Does scripture teach that God will make the wicked immortal, to suffer unending conscious torment in hell? Or does the Bible teach that the wicked will finally and truly die, perish, and become extinct forever, through *a destructive process that encompasses whatever degree and duration of conscious torment God might sovereignly and justly impose in each individual case?"* Edward Fudge

The traditionalist's doctrine of eternal life in agony and pain is *not* included in the universal Christian creeds and is rarely mentioned in statements of faith. Perhaps this is because the scriptural support is weak and the overwhelming evidence supports eternal destruction—a fire that consumes.

SUMMARY: Jesus's words to the traditionalists of His day can be read in Mark 2:25: "Have you not read . . ."

Perhaps this is quite appropriate for us today.

Believers are increasingly questioning the traditional view of Hell as both unbiblical and inconsistent with the character of God that lies primed for examination in every Bible found in homes everywhere.

Your rejection of this false notion of eternal agony for the lost should be a great relief. Your reception of conditionalism should come with comfort and a deep understanding that it is biblically sound. Our eternal life is conditional. The eternal life that God grants us is by His mercy through the finished work of Jesus Christ.

Your abandonment of this age-old view will provide a better understanding of God's Word and His character. Then you should develop an eagerness to undo this unsubstantiated and hideous slander of our Creator with everyone you know.

HELL PROVIDES ETERNAL PUNISH*MENT*—
NOT ETERNAL PUNISH*ING*.

Some Additional Resources

Websites and Podcasts:
    www.RethinkingHell.com (All of the podcasts are excellent.)
    www.beretta-online.com (Podcasts 005, 006, 007)
    www.EdwardFudge.com
    www.Afterlife.co.nz/
    www.Conditionalism.net
    www.TruthAccordingToScripture.com
    www.Conditionalism.net/blog

YouTube Videos:

"Traditional Objections [to Annihilationism] Answered, with
    Chris Date"
http://www.youtube.com/watch?v=OMxAYDlY9rQ
"William Lane Craig on Hell—Glenn Peoples"
http://www.youtube.com/watch?v=7VoSkxO2Omg
"The Case for Annihilationism, with Dr. Glenn Peoples"
http://www.youtube.com/watch?v=nrd1z8NXHFU
Melanie at the Indefatigable Theist, "Annihilationism and Eternal
    Hell"
http://www.youtube.com/watch?v=Vx44lCcddl8
"Ken Bussell—Pastor—The Case For Conditionalism"
http://www.youtube.com/watch?v=z-58McXzt_A

A Few of the Many Books Covering Conditional Immortality:
    The Fire That Consumes, Third Edition, by Edward Fudge
    Two Views of Hell by Edward Fudge and Robert Peterson
    Man's Ignorance and God's Grace by Roger Galstad
    What's The Truth About Heaven & Hell by Douglas Jacoby
    The Teaching of Jesus by Samuel G. Dawson
    Rescue From Death: John 3:16 Salvation by Dr. Robert Taylor
    Hell. A Final Word: The Surprising Truths I Found in the Bible by
    Edward Fudge

Challenge: Now, Read Your Bible with a New Perspective

If you will read through the Scriptures with an outlook somewhat modified by this book, I believe you will find that many tangled or confusing subjects will fit together and seem more straightforward than ever.

Every time I dig into God's Word, I'm amazed at the way it connects and makes more sense than it did before the ten subjects in this book became clear to me. Like clearing the vapor off a foggy window, the preconceived notions that I acquired from the traditionalism of our culture are gradually being removed—providing an unclouded perspective.

If you will allow the following requisites to penetrate your thinking before reading your Bible, I'm confident you will have the same experience of seeing God's Word weave together like a stunning and magnificent tapestry.

1) Understand that God is sovereignly in control of everything, while simultaneously using finite men and women, along with our good and bad decisions, to fulfill His perfect plan. All to His glory.

2) Look for the foreshadowing of God's amazing plan of redemption through His Son on the cross—the many prophecies and the "types and shadows" are unveiled throughout every book in the Old Testament.

3) Notice the clear teaching of man's mortality, from Genesis 3:22 all the way to the last book in the Bible, and the ultimate destruction of those who have not been brought to a place of repentance and faith by God's amazing mercy. Observe the clear teaching that eternal life is a gift given to those to whom God chooses to grant repentance and faith. Man's default setting is death and destruction, not eternal life in conscious agony.

4) Worship is about God, not us.

Thank you for investing your time in the reading of this book.

It is my hope that you will find the following appendices enjoyable and helpful.

APPENDIX A

SELECTED VERSES SHOWING THE SOVEREIGNTY OF GOD IN ALL THINGS, INCLUDING MAN'S SALVATION

"His Sovereignty rules over all."—Psalm 103:19

This list is a portion of a web-based compilation by David R. Sprenger.

Notes: All verses designated with the letter "P" refer specifically to predestination (the act of God predetermining and foreordaining that which will occur in order to fulfill His own purposes).

All verses designated with the letter "E" refer specifically to election ("The act of choice whereby God picks an individual or group out of a larger company for a purpose or destiny of His own appointment"—*The New Bible Dictionary).*

For quick reference, only the most obvious and specific verses pointing to predestination and election have been highlighted.

A personal note from David R. Sprenger: "I have been gathering these passages for over thirty years. I am always amazed and delighted that new ones are constantly being shown to me that previously went unnoticed, even though I've read and reread them many times before. I am beginning to believe there is almost no verse in the Bible that does not in some way declare the absolute sovereignty of God."

Old Testament Passages

P = Verses that tell us more of God's PREDESTINATION

E = Verses that tell us more of God's ELECTION

All others are verses that tell us more of God's SOVEREIGNTY

Genesis 1:1: In the beginning [literally, in beginnings] God created the heavens and the earth.

P: Genesis 12:3: And in you [Abraham] all the families of the earth shall be blessed.

P, E: Genesis 18:19: For I have chosen him, in order that he may command his children and his household after him to keep the way of the Lord by doing righteousness and justice; in order that the Lord may bring upon Abraham what He has spoken about him.

P: Genesis 50:20: And as for you, you meant evil against me, but God meant it for good in order to bring about this present result, to preserve many people alive. [Joseph speaking to his brothers who intended to kill him.]

P: Exodus 4:11: And the Lord said to him [Moses], "Who has made man's mouth? Or who makes him dumb or deaf, or seeing or blind? Is it not I, the Lord?"

P: Exodus 10:1-2: Then the Lord said to Moses, "Go to Pharaoh, for I have hardened his heart and the heart of his servants, that I may perform these signs of Mine among them . . . that you may know that I am the Lord."

E: Exodus 33:19: And I will be gracious to whom I will be gracious, and will show compassion on whom I will show compassion.

Numbers 14:20-21: So the Lord said, "I have pardoned them according to your word [Ed., Moses is represented here as a fore-type of Christ]; but indeed, as I live, all the earth will be filled with the glory of the Lord."

Deuteronomy 2:30: For the Lord your God hardened his [the king's] spirit and made his heart obstinate, in order to deliver him into your hand, as he is today.

E: Deuteronomy 7:6: For you are a holy people to the Lord your God; the Lord your God has chosen you to be a people for His own possession out of all the peoples who are on the face of the earth.

E: Deuteronomy 7:7-8: The Lord did not set His love on you nor choose you because you were more in number than any of the peoples, for you were the fewest of all peoples, but because the Lord loved you and kept the oath which He swore to your forefathers . . .

E: Deuteronomy 9:6: Know then, it is not because of your righteousness that the Lord your God is giving you this good land to possess, for you are a stubborn people.

E: Deuteronomy 9:24: You have been rebellious against the Lord from the day I knew you.

E: Deuteronomy 9:29: Yet they are Thy people, even Thine inheritance whom Thou hast brought out by Thy great power and Thine outstretched arm.

E: Deuteronomy 18:5: For the Lord your God has chosen him and his sons [the Levites] from all your tribes, to stand and serve in the name of the Lord forever.

E: Deuteronomy 29:4-6: Yet to this day the Lord has not given you a heart to know, nor eyes to see, nor ears to hear. Yet I have led you forty years in the wilderness; your clothes have not worn out on you, and your sandal has not worn out on your foot. You have not eaten bread, nor have you drunk wine or strong drink, in order that you might know that I am the Lord your God.

E: Deuteronomy 30:6: Moreover the Lord your God will circumcise your heart and the heart of your descendants, to love the Lord your God with all your heart and with all your soul, in order that you may live.

Deuteronomy 32:18: You neglected the Rock who begot you, and forgot the God who gave you birth.

P: Deuteronomy 32:39: See now that I, I am He, and there is no god besides Me; it is I who puts to death and gives life. I have wounded, and it is I who heals; and there is no one who can deliver from My hand.

P: Joshua 21:45: Not one of the good promises which the Lord had made to the house of Israel failed; all came to pass.

P: 1 Samuel 2:6-7: The Lord kills and makes alive; He brings down to Sheol and raises up. The Lord makes poor and rich; He brings low, He also exalts.

E: 1 Samuel 12:22: For the Lord will not abandon His people on account of His great name, because the Lord has been pleased to make you a people for Himself.

E: 2 Samuel 8:2: And he [David] defeated Moab, and measured them with the line, making them lie down on the ground; and he measured two lines to put to death and one full line to keep alive. And the Moabites became servants to David, bringing tribute. [Ed., A striking picture of God's choice and election!]

E: 1 Chronicles 28:4: Yet the Lord, the God of Israel, chose me from all the house of my fathers to be king over Israel forever.

2 Chronicles 18:33: And a certain man drew his bow at random [?!] and struck the king of Israel in a joint of the armor . . . And the battle raged that day . . . and at sunset he died.

2 Chronicles 20:6: Power and might are in Thy hand so that no one can stand against Thee.

E: 2 Chronicles 29:11: My sons [the Levites], do not be negligent now, for the Lord has chosen you to stand before Him, to minister to Him, and to be His ministers and burn incense.

P: Ezra 1:1: Now in the first year of Cyrus king of Persia, in order to fulfill the word of the Lord by the mouth of Jeremiah, the Lord stirred up the spirit of Cyrus king of Persia, so that he sent a proclamation throughout all his kingdom . . .

E: Nehemiah 9:7: Thou art the Lord God, who chose Abram and brought him out from Ur of the Chaldees, and gave him the name Abraham.

E: Nehemiah 11:1-2: Now the leaders of the people lived in Jerusalem, but the rest of the people cast lots to bring one out of ten to live in Jerusalem, the holy city, while nine-tenths remained in the other cities. And the people blessed all the men who volunteered to live in Jerusalem. [Ed., The Lord chooses; then you volunteer!]

P, E: Esther 4:14: For if you [Esther] remain silent at this time, relief and deliverance will arise for the Jews from another place and you and your father's house will perish. And who knows whether you have not attained royalty for such a time as this?

P: Job 1:1: And Job said, "Naked I came from my mother's womb, and naked I shall return there. The Lord gave and the Lord has taken away. Blessed be the name of the Lord."

P: Job 23:13-14: But He is unique and who can turn Him? And what His soul desires, that He does. For He performs what is appointed for me, and many such decrees are with Him.

P: Job 42:2: I know that Thou canst do all things, and that no purpose of Thine can be thwarted.

P, E: Psalm 2:7-8: I will surely tell of the decree of the Lord: He said to Me [Ed., prophetically speaking of Jesus], "Thou art my Son. Today I have begotten Thee. Ask of Me [The Father] and I will surely give the nations as Thine inheritance, and the very ends of the earth as Thy possession." [Ed., Notice this prophecy will also be fulfilled for the overcomers who are in the Son. See Rev. 2:27]

P: Psalm 16:6: The lines have fallen to me in pleasant places; indeed, my heritage is beautiful to me.

P, E: Psalm 22:9-10: Yet Thou art He who didst bring me forth from the womb; Thou didst make me trust when upon my mother's breasts. Upon Thee I was cast from birth; Thou hast been my God from my mother's womb.

P: Psalm 22:27-28: All the ends of the earth will remember and turn to the Lord, and all the families of the nations will worship before Thee. For the kingdom is the Lord's, and He rules over the nations.

Psalm 22:29: All the fat ones [Literally, proud ones] of the earth will eat and worship. All those who go down to the dust will bow before Him, even he who cannot keep his soul alive.

E: Psalm 33:12: Blessed is the nation whose God is the Lord, the people whom He has chosen for His own inheritance.

P: Psalm 33:14-15: From His dwelling place He looks out on all the inhabitants of the earth, He who fashions the hearts of them all, He who understands all their works.

E: Psalm 47:3-4: He subdues peoples under us, and nations under our feet. He chooses our inheritance for us, the glory of Jacob whom He loves.

P: Psalm 57:2: I will cry to God Most High, to God who accomplishes all things for me.

Psalm 65:2: To Thee all men [lit., all flesh] come.

E: Psalm 65:4: How blessed is the one whom Thou dost choose, and bring near to Thee.

P: Psalm 66:4: All the earth will worship Thee, and will sing praises to Thee; they will sing praises to Thy name.

Psalm 67:2, 7: That Thy way may be known on the earth, Thy salvation among all nations. God blesses us, that all the ends of the earth may fear Him.

Psalm 68:18: Thou hast ascended on high, Thou hast led captive Thy captives; Thou hast received gifts among men, even among the rebellious also, that the Lord God may dwell there.

Psalm 72:11, 19: And let all kings bow down before him, all nations serve Him . . . And may the whole earth be filled with His glory. Amen, and Amen.

Psalm 75:7: But God is the Judge; He puts down one, and exalts another.

P: Psalm 86:9: All nations whom Thou hast made shall come and worship before Thee, O Lord; and they shall glorify Thy name.

Psalm 100:3: Know that the Lord Himself is God; it is He who has made us, and not we ourselves; we are His people and the sheep of His pasture.

Psalm 103:9-10: He will not always strive with us; nor will He keep his anger forever. He has not dealt with us according to our sins, nor rewarded us according to our iniquities.

P: Psalm 103:19: The Lord has established His throne in the heavens; and His sovereignty rules over all.

P: Psalm 115:3: But our God is in the heavens; He does whatever He pleases.

Psalm 118:22: The stone which the builders rejected has become the chief corner stone. This is the Lord's doing; it is marvelous in our eyes.

Psalm 127:1: Unless the Lord builds the house, they labor in vain who build it. Unless the Lord guards the city, the watchman keeps awake in vain.

P: Psalm 130:8: And He will redeem Israel from all his iniquities.

P: Psalm 135:6: Whatever the Lord pleases, He does, in heaven and in earth, in seas and in all deeps.

P: Psalm 138:4: All the kings of the earth will give thanks to Thee, O Lord, when they have heard the words of Thy mouth. And they will sing of the ways of the Lord.

P: Psalm 138:8: The Lord will accomplish what concerns me.

Psalm 139:7-12: Where can I go from Thy Spirit? Or where can I flee from Thy presence?

P: Psalm 139:16: Thine eyes have seen my unformed substance; and in Thy book they were all written, the days that were ordained for me, when as yet there was not one of them.

Psalm 145:9: The Lord is good to all, and His mercies are over all His works.

P: Psalm 145:10: All Thy works shall give thanks to Thee, O Lord, and Thy godly ones shall bless Thee.

Psalm 145:14: The Lord sustains all who fall, and raises up all who are bowed down.

Psalm 145:15: The eyes of all look to Thee, and Thou dost give them their food in due time.

Psalm 145:16: Thou dost open Thy hand, and dost satisfy the desire of every living thing.

P: Psalm 145:21: My mouth will speak the praise of the Lord; and all flesh will bless His holy name forever and ever.

P: Psalm 148:8: Fire and hail, snow and clouds; stormy wind, fulfilling His word.

Proverbs 16:1: The plans of the heart belong to man, but the answer of the tongue is from the Lord.

P, E: Proverbs 16:4: The Lord has made everything for its own purpose, even the wicked for the day of evil.

P: Proverbs 16:9: The mind of man plans his way, but the Lord directs his steps.

P: Proverbs 16:33: The lot is cast into the lap, but its every decision is from the Lord.

P: Proverbs 19:21: Many are the plans in a man's heart, but the counsel of the Lord will be established.

P: Proverbs 20:24: Man's steps are ordained by the Lord; how then can man understand his way?

P: Proverbs 21:1: The king's heart is like channels of water in the hand of the Lord; He turns it wherever He wishes.

Proverbs 21:31: The horse is prepared for the day of battle, but victory belongs to the Lord.

P: Ecclesiastes 3:14: I know that everything God does will remain forever; there is nothing to add to it and there is nothing to take from it, for God has so worked that men should fear [be in awe of] Him.

P: Isaiah 2:2: In the last days the mountain of the house of the Lord will be established as the chief of the mountains, and will be raised above the hills; and all the nations will stream to it.

Isaiah 9:7: There will be no end to the increase of His government or of peace . . . from then on and forevermore. The zeal of the Lord of hosts will accomplish this.

P: Isaiah 10:5-7: Woe to Assyria, the rod of My anger and the staff in whose hands is My indignation. I send it against a godless nation . . . Yet it does not so intend nor does it plan so in its heart.

Isaiah 10:15: Is the axe to boast itself over the one who chops with it? Is the saw to exalt itself over the one who wields it? That would be like a club wielding those who lift it, or like a rod lifting him who is not wood.

P, E: Isaiah 10:22: For though your people, O Israel, may be like the sand of the sea, only a remnant within them will return; a destruction is determined, overflowing with righteousness.

P: Isaiah 11:9: They will not hurt or destroy in all My holy mountain, for the earth will be full of the knowledge of the Lord as the waters cover the sea.

P: Isaiah 14:24: The Lord of hosts has sworn saying, "Surely, just as I have intended so it has happened, and just as I have planned so it will stand."

P: Isaiah 14:27: For the Lord of hosts has planned, and who can frustrate it? And as for His stretched-out hand, who can turn it back?

P: Isaiah 19:17: And the land of Judah will become a terror to Egypt; everyone to whom it is mentioned will be in dread of it, because of the purpose of the Lord of hosts which He is purposing against them.

P: Isaiah 22:11: But you did not depend on Him who made it, nor did you take into consideration Him who planned it long ago.

P: Isaiah 23:9: The Lord of hosts has planned it to defile the pride of all beauty, to despise all the honored of the earth.

P: Isaiah 25:7-8: And on this mountain He will swallow up the covering which is over all peoples, even the veil which is stretched over all nations. He will swallow up death for all time, and the Lord will wipe tears away from all faces, and He will remove the reproach of His people from all the earth; for the Lord has spoken.

Isaiah 26:9: For when the earth experiences Thy judgements, the inhabitants of the world learn righteousness. [Ed., The ultimate purpose of God's judgements is to learn, not burn!]

P: Isaiah 26:12: Lord, Thou wilt establish peace for us, since Thou hast also performed for us all our works.

Isaiah 27:3: I, the Lord, am [the vineyard's] keeper; I water it every moment, lest anyone damage it; I guard it night and day.

P: Isaiah 40:5: Then the glory of the Lord will be revealed, and all flesh will see it together; for the mouth of the Lord has spoken.

P: Isaiah 43:13: Even from eternity I am He; and there is none who can deliver out of My hand; I act and who can reverse it?

E: Isaiah 43:20: Because I have given waters in the wilderness and rivers in the desert, to give drink to My chosen people. The people whom I formed for Myself, will declare My praise.

E: Isaiah 45:4-5: For the sake of Jacob My servant, and Israel My chosen one, I have called you [Cyrus, King of Persia] by your name. I have given you a title of honor though you have not known Me . . . I will gird you though you have not known Me. [Ed., Cyrus was an unbelieving Gentile ruler. Although sympathetic to the Israelites, by decree he helped restore all the other false deities to their renovated temples.]

P: Isaiah 45:6-7: There is no one besides Me. I am the Lord, and there is no other, the One forming light and creating darkness, causing well being and creating calamity [Lit., "ra," evil]. I am the Lord who does all these.

Isaiah 45:12: It is I who made the earth, and created man upon it. I stretched out the heavens with My hands, and I ordained all their host.

E: Isaiah 45:17: Israel has been saved by the Lord with an everlasting salvation; you will not be put to shame or humiliated to all eternity.

P: Isaiah 45:22-23: Turn to Me and be saved, all the ends of the earth; for I am God, and there is no other. I have sworn by Myself, the word has gone forth from My mouth in righteousness and will not turn back, that to Me every knee will bow, every tongue will swear allegiance.

P, E: Isaiah 46:9-11: For I am God, and there is no other; I am God, and there is no one like Me, declaring the end from the beginning and from ancient times things which have not been done, saying, "My purpose will be established, and I will accomplish all My good pleasure"; calling a bird of prey from the east, the man of My purpose from a far country.

Truly I have spoken; truly I will bring it to pass. I have planned it, surely I will do it.

Isaiah 48:11: For My own sake, for My own sake, I will act; for how can My name be profaned? And My glory I will not give to another.

E: Isaiah 48:12: Listen to me, O Jacob, even Israel whom I called; I am He, I am the first, I am also the last.

P: Isaiah 53:6: All of us like sheep have gone astray, each of us has turned to his own way; but the Lord has caused the iniquity of us all to fall on Him.

Isaiah 54:16: Behold, I Myself have created the smith who blows the fire of coals, and brings out a weapon for its work; and I have created the destroyer to ruin. No weapon that is formed against you shall prosper.

P: Isaiah 55:11: So shall my word be which goes forth from My mouth; it shall not return to Me empty, without accomplishing what I desire, and without succeeding in the matter for which I sent it.

P, E: Isaiah 57:17-18: Because of the iniquity of his unjust gain I was angry and struck him; I hid my face and was angry, and he went on turning away, in the way of his heart. I have seen his ways, but I will heal him; I will lead him and restore comfort to him and to his mourners creating the praise of the lips.

Isaiah 59:15-16: Now the Lord saw, and it was displeasing in His sight that there was no justice. And He saw that there was no man, and was astonished that there was no one to intercede; then His own arm brought salvation to Him; and His righteousness upheld Him.

P, E: Isaiah 60:21: Then all your people [all Israel] will be righteous; they will possess the land forever, the branch of My planting, the work of My hands, that I may be glorified.

P: Isaiah 60:22: The smallest one will become a clan, and the least one a mighty nation. I, the Lord, will hasten it in its time.

Isaiah 61:11: For as the earth brings forth its sprouts, and as a garden causes the things sown in it to spring up, so the Lord God will cause righteousness and praise to spring up before all the nations.

Isaiah 63:17: Why, O Lord, dost Thou cause us to stray from Thy ways, and harden our heart from fearing Thee? Return for the sake of Thy servants, the tribes of Thy heritage.

E: Isaiah 65:1: I permitted Myself to be sought by those who did not ask for Me; I permitted Myself to be found by those who did not seek Me. I said, "Here am I, here am I," to a nation which did not call on My name.

Isaiah 66:1: Thus says the Lord, "Heaven is My throne, and earth is My footstool. Where then is a house you could build for Me? And where is a place that I may rest? For My hand made all these things; thus all these things came into being," declares the Lord.

P: Isaiah 66:18, 23: For I know their works and their thoughts; the time is coming to gather all nations and tongues. And they shall come and see My glory . . . All mankind [lit., all flesh] will come to bow down before Me, says the Lord.

P, E: Jeremiah 1:5: Before I formed you in the womb I knew you, and before you were born I consecrated you; I have appointed you a prophet to the nations.

P: Jeremiah 4:28: Because I have spoken, I have purposed, and I will not change My mind [lit. be sorry], nor will I turn from it.

P: Jeremiah 10:23: I know, O Lord, that a man's way is not in himself; nor is it in a man who walks to direct his steps.

Jeremiah 16:21: Therefore behold, I am going to make them know—this time I will make them know My power and My might; and they shall know that My name is the Lord.

Jeremiah 18:11: Thus says the Lord, "I am fashioning evil [Heb. "ra"] against you [His chosen people] and devising a plan against you. Oh turn back, each of you from his evil way, and reform your ways and your deeds." [Ed., God uses evil for the purpose of helping initiate reform.]

P, E: Jeremiah 23:3: Then I Myself shall gather the remnant of My flock out of all the countries where I have driven them and shall bring them back to their pasture; and they will be fruitful and multiply.

Jeremiah 23:24: "Can a man hide himself in hiding places, so I do not see him?" declares the Lord. "Do I not fill the heavens and the earth?" declares the Lord.

P, E: Jeremiah 24:7: And I will give them a heart to know Me, for I am the Lord; and they will be My people, and I will be their God, for they will return to Me with their whole heart.

E: Jeremiah 27:5: I have made the earth, the men and the beasts which are on the face of the earth by My great power and by My outstretched arm, and I will give it to the one who is pleasing in My sight.

P: Jeremiah 29:11-12: "For I know the plans that I have for you," declares the Lord, "plans for welfare and not for calamity to give you a future and a hope." Then you will call upon Me and come and pray to Me, and I will listen to you . . ."

E: Jeremiah 31:1, 3: "At that time," declares the Lord, "I will be the God of all the families of Israel, and they shall be My people . . . I have loved you with an everlasting love. Therefore I have drawn you with lovingkindness."

E: Jeremiah 31:33: "But this is the covenant which I will make with the house of Israel after those days," declares the Lord. "I will put My law within them, and on their heart I will write it; and I will be their God, and they shall be My people."

Jeremiah 31:34: "And they shall not teach again, each man his neighbor and each man his brother, saying, 'Know the Lord,' for they shall all know Me, from the least of them to the greatest of them," declares the Lord, "for I will forgive their iniquity, and their sin I will remember no more."

Jeremiah 32:27: Behold, I am the Lord, the God of all flesh; is anything too difficult for Me?

Jeremiah 32:40: And I will make an everlasting covenant with them that I will not turn away from them, to do them good; and I will put the fear [awe] of Me in their hearts so that they will not turn away from Me.

E: Jeremiah 46:28: For I shall make a full end of all the nations where I have driven you [Israel], yet I shall not make a full end of you; but I shall correct you properly and by no means leave you unpunished. [Ed., God's punishments are always for correction, and are therefore remedial, not vindictive.]

P: Jeremiah 51:12: For the Lord has both purposed and performed what He spoke concerning the inhabitants . . .

P: Lamentations 2:17: The Lord has done what He purposed; He has accomplished His word which He commanded from days of old.

Lamentations 3:31: For the Lord will not reject forever, for if He causes grief, then He will have compassion according to His abundant lovingkindness.

P: Lamentations 3:37-39: Who is there who speaks and it comes to pass, unless the Lord has commanded it? Is it not from the mouth of the Most

High that both good and evil go forth? Why should any living mortal, or any man, offer complaint in view of his sins?

Ezekiel 7:9: I will repay you according to your ways, while your abominations are in your midst; then you will know that I, the Lord, do the smiting.

P: Ezekiel 12:25: For I the Lord shall speak, and whatever word I speak will be performed.

P: Ezekiel 20:44: Then you will know that I am the Lord when I have dealt with you for My name's sake, not according to your evil ways or according to your corrupt deeds, O house of Israel, declares the Lord God.

P: Ezekiel 24:14: I, the Lord, have spoken; it is coming and I shall act.

P, E: Ezekiel 36:22-27: Therefore, say to the house of Israel, "Thus says the Lord God, 'It is not for your sake, O house of Israel, that I am about to act, but for My holy name, which you have profaned among the nations where you went . . . Then the nations will know that I am the Lord, declares the Lord God, when I prove Myself holy among you in their sight. For I will take you from the nations, gather you from all the lands, and bring you into your own land. Then I will sprinkle clean water on you and you will be clean; I will cleanse you from all your filthiness and from all your idols. Moreover, I will give you a new heart and put a new spirit within you; and I will remove the heart of stone from your flesh and give you a heart of flesh. And I will put My Spirit within you and cause you to walk in My statutes, and you will be careful to observe My ordinances.'"

E: Ezekiel 36:31-32: "Then you will remember your evil ways and your deeds that were not good, and you will loathe yourselves in your own sight for your iniquities and your abominations. I am not doing this for your sake," declares the Lord God, "let it be known to you. Be ashamed and confounded for your ways, O house of Israel!"

Ezekiel 37:5: Thus says the Lord God to these bones, "Behold, I will cause breath to enter you that you may come to life." [Ed., This points to Jesus saying, "I am the resurrection and the life." (Jn. 11:25) Also Paul states, "And even when you were dead in your transgressions and the uncircumcision of your flesh, He made you alive together with Him, having forgiven us all our transgressions. (Col. 2:13; Ephes. 2:4, 5)]

Ezekiel 37:14: "And I will put My Spirit within you, and you will come to life, and I will place you on your own land. Then you will know that I, the Lord, have spoken and done it," declares the Lord.

Ezekiel 38:23: And I shall magnify Myself, sanctify Myself, and make Myself known in the sight of many nations; and they will know that I am the Lord. [Ed., This phrase is used literally dozens of times throughout Ezekiel and throughout all of Scripture. It is the basis for all of God's sovereign dealings with man, and reveals His ultimate goal and intention: "That I may know Him . . ." (Phil 3:10), "And this is eternal life, that they may know Thee, the only true God, and Jesus Christ whom Thou hast sent" (Jn 17:3).]

P, E: Daniel 2: 21: And it is He who changes the times and the epochs; He removes kings and establishes kings; He gives wisdom to wise men, and knowledge to men of understanding.

P: Daniel 2:44: And in the days of those kings, the God of heaven will set up a kingdom which will never be destroyed, and that kingdom will not be left for another people; it will crush and put an end to all these kingdoms, but it will itself endure forever.

Daniel 4:3: How great are His signs, and how great are His wonders! His kingdom is an everlasting kingdom, and His dominion is from generation to generation.

P: Daniel 4:35: And all the inhabitants of the earth are accounted as nothing, but He does according to His will in the Host of heaven and among the inhabitants of earth; and no one can ward off His hand or say to Him, "What hast Thou done."

P: Daniel 5:23 But the God in whose hand are your life-breath and your ways, you have not glorified.

Daniel 7:13-14: I kept looking in the night visions, and behold, with the clouds of heaven One like a Son of Man was coming, and He came up to the Ancient of Days and was presented before Him. And to Him was given dominion, glory, and a kingdom, that all the peoples, nations, and men of every language might serve Him. His kingdom is an everlasting kingdom which will not pass away; and His kingdom is one which will not be destroyed.

Daniel 7:27: Then the sovereignty, the dominion, and the greatness of all the kingdoms under the whole heaven will be given to the people of the saints of the Highest One; His kingdom will be an everlasting kingdom, and all the dominions will serve and obey Him.

P: Daniel 11:36: For that which is decreed will be done.

E: Hosea 13:14: I will ransom them from the power of Sheol; I will redeem them from death. O death, where are your thorns? O Sheol, where is your sting?

Hosea 14:4: I will heal their apostasy, I will love them freely, for My anger has turned away from them.

P, E: Joel 2:26-32: And you shall have plenty to eat and be satisfied, and praise the name of the Lord your God, who has dealt wondrously with you; then My people will never be put to shame. Thus you will know that I am in the midst of Israel, and that I am the Lord your God and there is no other; and My people will never be put to shame. And it will come about after this that I will pour out My Spirit on all mankind; and your sons and daughters will prophesy, your old men will dream dreams, your young men will see visions . . . For on Mount Zion and in Jerusalem there will be those who escape, as the Lord has said, even among the survivors whom the Lord calls.

P: Amos 3:6-8: If calamity [lit. "ra," evil] occurs in a city has not the Lord done it? Surely the Lord God does nothing unless He reveals His secret counsel to His servants the prophets. A lion has roared! Who will not fear? The Lord God has spoken! Who can but prophesy?

Amos 4:13: For behold, He who forms mountains and creates the wind and declares to man what are His thoughts, He who makes dawn into darkness and treads on the high places of the earth, The Lord God of hosts is His name.

Jonah 2:9: Salvation is from the Lord.

E: Micah 4:6-7: In that day, declares the Lord, I will assemble the lame, and gather the outcasts, even those whom I have afflicted. I will make the lame a remnant, and the outcasts a strong nation, and the Lord will reign over them in Mount Zion from now on and forever.

P, E: Micah 5:2: But as for you, Bethlehem Ephrathah, too little to be among the clans of Judah, from you One will go forth for Me to be ruler in Israel. His goings forth are from long ago, from the days of eternity.

Micah 7:18-20: Who is a God like Thee, who pardons iniquity and passes over the rebellious act of the remnant of His possession? He does not retain His anger forever, because He delights in unchanging love. He will again have compassion on us; He will tread our iniquities underfoot. Yes, Thou wilt cast all our sins into the depths of the sea. Thou wilt give truth to Jacob and unchanging love to Abraham, which Thou didst swear to our forefathers from the days of old.

Habakkuk 2:14: For the earth will be filled with the knowledge of the Lord, as the waters cover the sea.

E: Habakkuk 3:12-13: In indignation Thou didst march through the earth; in anger Thou didst trample [thresh] the nations. Thou didst go forth for the salvation of Thy people, for the salvation of Thine anointed. Thou didst strike the head of the house of the evil to lay him open from thigh to neck.

Habakkuk 3:19: The Lord God is my strength, and He has made my feet like hinds' feet, and makes me walk on high places.

P: Zephaniah 2:11: The Lord will be terrifying to them, for He will starve all the gods of the earth; and all the coastlands of the nations will bow down to Him, every one from his own place.

Zephaniah 3:8-9: Indeed, My decision is to gather nations, to assemble kingdoms, to pour out on them My indignation, all My burning anger; for all the earth will be devoured by the fire of My zeal. For then I will give to the peoples purified lips, that all of them may call on the name of the Lord, to serve Him shoulder to shoulder. [Ed., Note that the purpose of God's fire and indignation is for purification, that is, ". . . though they are judged in the flesh as men, they may live in the spirit according to the will of God" (1 Peter 4:6).]

Haggai 2:6-7: For thus says the Lord of hosts, "Once more in a little while, I am going to shake the heavens and the earth, the sea also and the dry land. And I will shake all the nations; and they will come with all the wealth of the nations; and I will fill this house with glory," says the Lord of hosts.

Haggai 2:21-22: I am going to shake the heavens and the earth. And I will overthrow the thrones of kingdoms and destroy the power of the kingdoms of the nations; and I will overthrow the chariots and their riders, and the horses and their riders will go down, every one by the sword of another.

P: Zechariah 2:10-11: Sing for joy and be glad, O daughter of Zion; for behold I am coming and I will dwell in your midst, declares the Lord.

And many nations will join themselves to the Lord in that day and will become My people. Then I will dwell in your midst, and you will know that the Lord of hosts has sent Me to you.

E: Zechariah 3:1-4: Then he showed me Joshua the high priest standing before the angel of the Lord, and Satan standing at his right hand to accuse him. And the Lord said to Satan, "The Lord rebuke you, Satan! Indeed, the Lord who has chosen Jerusalem rebuke you! Is this not a brand plucked from the fire?" Now Joshua was clothed with filthy garments and standing before the angel. And he spoke and said to those who were standing before him saying, "Remove the filthy garments from him." Again he said to him, "See, I have taken your iniquity away from you and will clothe you with festal robes."

E: Zechariah 4:6-7: Then he answered and said to me, "This is the word of the Lord to Zerubbabel saying, 'Not by might nor by power, but by My Spirit,' says the Lord or hosts. 'What are you, O great mountain? Before Zerubbabel you will become a plain; and he will bring forth the top stone with shouts of 'Grace, grace to it!'"

P, E: Zechariah 8:12-13: And I will cause the remnant of this people to inherit all these things. And it will come about that just as you were a curse among the nations, O house of Judah and house of Israel, so I will save you that you may become a blessing. Do not fear. Let your hands be strong.

Zechariah 9:10: And He will speak peace to the nations; and His dominion will be from sea to sea, and from the River [i.e., the Euphrates] to the ends of the earth.

Zechariah 14:8-9: And it will come about in that day that living waters will flow out of Jerusalem, half of them toward the eastern sea and the other half toward the western sea; it will be in summer as well as in winter. And the Lord will be king over all the earth; in that day the Lord will be one, and His name one. [Some trans. add, "the only one."]

Malachi 1:11 For from the rising of the sun, even to its setting, My name will be great among the nations, and in every place incense is going to be offered to My name, and a grain offering that is pure; for My name will be great among the nations, says the Lord of hosts.

New Testament Passages

P = Verses that tell us more of God's PREDESTINATION

E = Verses that tell us more of God's ELECTION

All others are verses that tell us more of God's SOVEREIGNTY

P: Matthew 10:29-30: Are not two sparrows sold for a penny? Yet not one of them will fall to the ground apart from the will of your Father. And even the very hairs on your head are numbered. (NIV)

E: Matthew 11:25-27: And no one knows the Father except the Son and those to whom the Son chooses to reveal Him.

E: Matthew 13:11: To you it has been granted to know the mysteries of the kingdom of Heaven, but to them it has not been granted.

E: Matthew 15:13: Every plant which my heavenly Father did not plant shall be rooted up.

P: Matthew 18:14: Thus it is not the will of your Father who is in heaven that one of these little ones perish.

E: Matthew 19:11: Jesus replied, "Not everyone can accept this teaching, but only those to whom it has been given." (NIV)

Matthew 19:26: With man this [salvation] is impossible, but with God all things are possible. (NIV)

P, E: Matthew 20:23: This is not Mine to give, but it is for those for whom it has been prepared by My Father.

E: Matthew 22:14: For many are called, but few are chosen.

E: Matthew 24:22: But for the sake of the elect those days shall be cut short.

P: Matthew 26:54: But how then would the Scriptures be fulfilled that say it must happen in this way? (NIV)

E: Mark 4:10-12: To you has been given the mystery of the kingdom of God; but those who are outside get everything in parables . . . lest they return again and be forgiven.

E: Mark 13:20: But for the sake of the elect whom He chose, He shortened the days.

P: Luke 1:20: And behold, you shall be silent and unable to speak until the day when these things take place, because you did not believe my words, which shall be fulfilled in their proper time.

E: Luke 8:10: To you it has been granted to know the mysteries of the kingdom of God, but to the rest it is in parables; in order that seeing they may not see, and hearing they may not understand.

E: Luke 10:21-22: No one knows who the Father is except the Son . . . and anyone to whom the Son wills to reveal Him.

Luke 18:26-27: Those who heard this asked, "Who then can be saved?" Jesus replied, "What is impossible with men is possible with God." (NIV)

Luke 20:38: For all live to Him.

P, E: John 1:12-13 Who were born not of blood, nor of the will of the flesh, nor of the will of man, but of [the will of] God.

E: John 3:27: A man can receive nothing unless it has been given him from heaven.

E: John 5:21: The Son also gives life to whom He wishes [Greek: wills].

John 5:25: The dead shall hear the voice of the Son of God, and those who hear shall live.

E: John 6:37: All that the Father gives Me shall come to Me.

E: John 6:39: And this is the will of Him who sent Me, that of all that He has given Me I lose nothing, but raise it up on the last day.

E: John 6:44: No one can come to Me unless the Father who sent Me draws him.

E: John 6:65: For this reason I have said to you, that no one can come to Me unless it has been granted him from the Father.

John 8:36: If therefore the Son shall make you free, you shall be free indeed.

John 8:43: Why do you not understand what I am saying? It is because you cannot hear My word.

John 10:16: I must bring them also, and they shall hear My voice; and they shall become one flock with one shepherd.

John 10:27-28: And I give eternal life to them [my sheep], and they shall never perish and no one shall snatch them out of My hand.

John 11:43: He cried out with a loud voice, "Lazarus, come forth." He who had died came forth . . .

John 12:32: And if I be lifted up from the earth, I will draw all men to Myself.

John 12:39-40: For this cause they could not believe, for Isaiah said again, "He has blinded their eyes and He hardened their heart; lest they see with their eyes and perceive with their heart, and be converted, and I heal them."

E: John 13:18: I do not speak of all of you. I know the ones I have chosen.

E: John 15:16: You did not choose Me, but I chose you, and appointed you, that you should go and bear fruit and that your fruit should remain.

E: John 15:19: But because you are not of the world, but I chose you out of the world, therefore the world hates you.

E: John 17:2: Even as Thou gavest Him authority over all mankind, that to all whom Thou hast given Him, He may give eternal life.

E: John 17:6: I manifested Thy name to the men whom Thou gavest Me out of the world.

E: John 17:9: I ask on their behalf; I do not ask on behalf of the world, but of those whom Thou hast given Me; for they are Thine.

John 19:11: You would have no authority over me, unless it had been given you from above.

E: Acts 1:2: After he had by the Holy Spirit given orders to the apostles whom He had chosen.

P: Acts 1:16: Brethren, the scripture had to be fulfilled, which the Holy Spirit foretold by the mouth of David . . .

P: Acts 2:23: This Man, delivered up by the predetermined plan and the foreknowledge of God, you nailed to a cross by the hands of godless men . . .

E: Acts 2:39: For the promise is for you and your children, and for all who are far off, as many as the Lord our God shall call to Himself.

Acts 3:26: . . . and sent Him to bless you by turning every one of you from your wicked ways.

P: Acts 4:27-28: For truly in this city there were gathered together against Thy holy servant Jesus, whom Thou didst anoint, both Herod and Pontius Pilate, along with the Gentiles and the peoples of Israel, to do whatever Thy hand and Thy purpose predestined to occur.

Acts 5:31: He is the One whom God exalted to His right hand as a Prince and a Savior, to grant repentance to Israel, and forgiveness of sins. [Ed. He grants the repentance as well as the forgiveness.]

E: Acts 9:15: For he [Paul] is a chosen instrument of Mine to bear My name before the Gentiles . . .

P, E: Acts 10:40-41: God raised Him up on the third day, and granted that He should become visible, not to all the people, but to witnesses who were chosen beforehand by God.

Acts 11:18: God has granted to the Gentiles also the repentance that leads to life. [Ed., Again, repentance is granted by God.]

P, E: Acts 13:48: And as many as had been appointed [ordained] to eternal life believed.

E: Acts 15:7: In the early days God made a choice among you, that by my mouth [Peter's] the Gentiles should hear the word of the gospel and believe.

Acts 15:9: And He made no distinction between us [Jews] and them [Gentiles], cleansing their hearts by faith. [Ed., God cleanses the heart, and He does so by granting us faith.]

Acts 15:11: But we believe that we are saved through the grace of the Lord Jesus, in the same way as they also are.

E: Acts 16:14: And the Lord opened her heart to respond to the things spoken by Paul.

P: Acts 17:26-28: And He made from one, every nation of mankind to live on all the face of the earth, having determined their appointed times, and the boundaries of their habitation . . . for in Him we live and move and are.

Acts 17:30: Therefore having overlooked the times of ignorance, God is now declaring to men that all everywhere should repent.

Acts 18:27: On arriving, he [Paul] was a great help to those who by grace had believed. (NIV) [Ed. No one can believe apart from receiving God's sovereign grace.]

P: Acts 22:10: Arise and go on into Damascus; and there you will be told of all that has been appointed for you to do.

E: Acts 22:14: The God of our fathers has appointed you to know His will, and to see the Righteous One, and to hear an utterance from His mouth.

Romans 2:4: Or do you think lightly of the riches of His kindness and forbearance and patience, not knowing that the kindness of God leads you to repentance?

Romans 3:23-24 For all have sinned and fall short [Greek present tense: are sinning and falling short] of the glory of God, being justified [Greek present passive tense] as a gift by His grace through the redemption which is in Christ Jesus.

E: Romans 4:17: Even God, who gives life to the dead and calls into being that which does not exist.

Romans 4:21: And being fully assured that what He had promised, He was able also to perform.

Romans 5:6: For while we were still helpless, at the right time Christ died for the ungodly.

Romans 5:8: But God demonstrates His own love toward us, in that while we were yet sinners, Christ died for us.

Romans 5:10: For if while we were enemies, we were reconciled to God through the death of His Son, much more, having been reconciled, we shall be saved by his life.

Romans 5:15: But the free gift is not like the transgression. For if by the transgression of the one [Adam] the many died, much more did the grace of God and the gift by the grace of the one Man, Jesus Christ, abound to the many.

Romans 5:18: So then as through one transgression there resulted condemnation to all men, even so through one act of righteousness there resulted justification of life to all men.

Romans 5:19: For as through the one man's [Adam's] disobedience the many were made sinners, even so through the obedience of the One the many will be made righteous.

Romans 5:20: And the law came in that the transgression might increase; but where sin increased, grace abounded all the more.

Romans 5:19: For the anxious longing of the creation waits eagerly for the revealing of the sons of God.

P: Romans 8:20-21: For the creation was subjected to futility, not of its own will, but because of Him who subjected it in hope that the creation itself also will be set free from its slavery to corruption into the freedom of the glory of the children of God.

P, E: Romans 8:28: And we know that God causes all things to work together for good to those who love God, to those who are called according to His purpose.

P, E: Romans 8:29: For whom He foreknew, He also predestined to become conformed to the image of His Son, that He might be the firstborn among many brethren.

P, E: Romans 8:30: And whom He predestined, these He also called; and whom He called, these He also justified; and whom He justified, these He also glorified.

Romans 8:31: What then shall we say to these things? If God is for us who is against us?

E: Romans 8:33: Who will bring a charge against God's elect? God is the one who justifies.

E: Romans 9:11: For though the twins were not yet born, and had not done anything good or bad, in order that God's purpose according to His choice might stand, not because of works, but because of Him who calls . . .

E: Romans 9:16: So then it does not depend on the man who wills or the man who runs, but on God who has mercy.

E: Romans 9:18: So then He has mercy on whom He desires, and He hardens whom He desires.

Romans 9:19: You will say to me then, "Why does He still find fault? For who can resist His will?"

P: Romans 9:20: On the contrary, who are you, O man, who answers back to God? The thing molded will not say to the molder, "Why did you make me like this," will it?

P, E: Romans 9:21: Or does not the potter have a right over the clay, to make from the same lump one vessel for honor, and another for dishonor?

P: Romans 9:22: What if God, although willing to demonstrate His wrath and to make His power known, endured with much patience vessels of wrath prepared for destruction?

P, E: Romans 9:23: In order that He might make known the riches of His glory upon vessels of mercy, which He prepared beforehand for glory.

E: Romans 9:24: Even us, whom He also called, not from among Jews only, but also from among Gentiles.

E: Romans 9:27: And Isaiah cries out concerning Israel, "Though the number of the sons of Israel be as the sand of the sea, it is the remnant that will be saved."

E: Romans 11:5: In the same way then, there has also come to be at the present time a remnant according to God's gracious choice [Lit., God's choice of grace].

P, E: Romans 11:26: And thus all Israel will be saved; just as it is written, "The Deliverer will come from Zion, and He will remove ungodliness from Jacob."

Romans 11:27: "And this is My covenant with them, when I take away their sins."

E: Romans 11:28: From the standpoint of the gospel they are enemies for your sake, but from the standpoint of God's choice they are beloved for the sake of the fathers.

E: Romans 11:29: For the gifts and the calling of God are irrevocable.

Romans 11:32: For God has shut up all men in disobedience that He may show mercy to all.

Romans 11:33: Oh, the depth of the riches both of the wisdom and knowledge of God! How unsearchable are His judgements and unfathomable His ways!

Romans 11:36: For from Him and through Him and to Him are all things. To Him be the glory forever. Amen.

Romans 14:4: Who are you to judge the servant of another? To his own master he stands or falls; and stand he will, for the Lord is able to make him stand.

E: 1 Corinthians 1:1: Paul, called as an apostle of Jesus Christ by the will of God . . .

E: 1 Corinthians 1:27-29: But God has chosen the foolish things of the world to shame the wise . . . that no man should boast before God.

E: 1 Corinthians 1:30: But by His doing (Lit., of Him) you are in Christ Jesus . . .

E: 1 Corinthians 4:7: For who regards you as superior? And what do you have that you did not receive?

1 Corinthians 9:16-17: For if I preach the gospel, I have nothing to boast of, for I am under compulsion; for woe is me if I do not preach the gospel. For if I do this voluntarily, I have a reward; but if against my will, I have a stewardship entrusted to me.

1 Corinthians 12:11: But one and the same Spirit works all these things, distributing to each one individually just as He wills.

1 Corinthians 15:10: But by the grace of God I am what I am, and His grace toward me did not prove vain; but I labored even more than all of them, yet not I, but the grace of God with me.

2 Corinthians 1:1: Paul, an apostle of Christ Jesus by the will of God . . .

2 Corinthians 4:6: For God, who said, "Light shall shine out of darkness," is the One who has shone in our hearts to give the light of the knowledge of the glory of God in the face of Christ.

2 Corinthians 5:14: For the love of Christ controls us, having concluded this, that one died for all, therefore all died.

E: 2 Corinthians 5:17-19: Therefore if any man is in Christ, he is a new creature; the old things passed away; behold new things have come. Now all these things are from God who reconciled us to Himself through Christ, and gave us the ministry of reconciliation, namely, that God was in Christ reconciling the world to Himself, not counting their trespasses against them, and He has committed [Lit., placed in us] the word of reconciliation.

2 Corinthians 7:9: For you were made sorrowful according to the will of God, in order that you might not suffer loss in anything through us.

2 Corinthians 7:10: For the sorrow that is according to the will of God produces a repentance without regret, leading to salvation; but sorrow of the world produces death.

2 Corinthians 8:5: But they [the saints in Macedonia] first gave themselves to the Lord and to us by the will of God.

Galatians 1:4: Who gave Himself for our sins, that He might deliver us out of this present evil age, according to the will of our God and Father.

P, E: Galatians 1:15-16: But when He who had set me apart from my mother's womb, and called me through His grace, was pleased to reveal His Son in me . . .

P: Galatians 3:8: And the Scripture, foreseeing that God would justify the nations by faith, preached the gospel beforehand to Abraham, saying, "All the nations shall be blessed in you."

E: Galatians 4:9: But now that you have come to know God, or rather to be known by God.

Galatians 5:1: It was for freedom that Christ set us free . . .

E: Ephesians 1:1: Paul, an apostle of Christ Jesus by the will of God . . .

P, E: Ephesians 1:4: Just as He chose us in Him before the foundation of the world . . .

P, E: Ephesians 1:5-6: He predestined us to adoption as sons through Jesus Christ to Himself, according to the kind intention of His will, to the praise of the glory of His grace . . .

P: Ephesians 1:9-10: And He made known to us the mystery of His will according to His good pleasure, which He purposed in Christ to put into effect when the times will have reached their fulfillment—to bring all things in heaven and on earth together [the summing up of all things, NAS] under one head, even Christ. [NIV]

P: Ephesians 1:11: In whom also we have obtained an inheritance, having been predestined according to His purpose who works all things after the counsel of His will.

P, E: Ephesians 2:4-5: But God, being rich in mercy, because of His great love with which He loved us, even when we were dead in our transgressions, made us alive together with Christ (by grace you have been saved).

E: Ephesians 2:8-9: For by grace you have been saved through faith; and that [faith] not of yourselves, it is a gift of God; not as a result of works, that no one should boast.

P: Ephesians 2:10: For we are His workmanship, created in Christ Jesus for good works, which God prepared beforehand, that we should walk in them.

P: Ephesians 3:11: This was in accordance with the eternal purpose [Lit., purpose of the ages] which He carried out in Christ Jesus our Lord.

Ephesians 4:6: One God and Father of all who is over all and through all and in all.

Ephesians 4:10: He who descended is Himself also He who ascended far above all the heavens, that He might fill all things.

P: Philippians 1:6: For I am confident of this very thing, that He who began a good work in you will perfect it until the day of Christ Jesus.

E: Philippians 1:29: For to you it has been granted for Christ's sake, not only to believe in Him, but also to suffer for His sake.

P: Philippians 2:9-11: Therefore also God highly exalted Him, and bestowed on Him the name which is above every name, that at the name of Jesus every knee should bow, of those who are in heaven, and on earth, and under the earth, and that every tongue should confess that Jesus Christ is Lord, to the glory of God the Father. [See Isaiah 45:22-23 for original context!]

Philippians 2:12-13: Work out [Strong's Concordance: effect or engage in] your salvation with fear and trembling; for it is God who is at work in you, both to will and to work for His good pleasure.

Philippians 3:21: Who will transform our lowly body into conformity with His glorious body, by the exertion of the power that He has even to subject all things to Himself.

E: Colossians 1:1: Paul, an apostle of Jesus Christ by the will of God . . .

Colossians 1:13: For He delivered us from the domain of darkness, and transferred us to the kingdom of the Son of His love.

Colossians 1:15: And He is the image of the invisible God, the firstborn of [Greek, *protokos:* prior to and sovereign over] all creation.

P: Colossians 1:16-18: For in Him all things were created . . . all things have been created through Him and for Him. And He is before all things, and in Him all things hold together . . . so that He Himself might come to have first place [i.e., preeminence] in all things.

Colossians 1:19-20: For it was the Father's good pleasure for all the fulness to dwell in Him, and through Him to reconcile all things to Himself, having made peace through the blood of His cross; through Him, I say, whether things on earth or things in heaven.

Colossians 2:13: And when you were dead in your transgressions and the uncircumcision of your flesh, He made you alive together with Him, having forgiven us all our transgressions.

Colossians 3:11: Christ is all, and in all.

E: Colossians 3:12: And so, as those who have been chosen of God, holy and beloved, put on a heart of compassion, kindness, humility, gentleness . . .

E: 1 Thessalonians 1:4: Knowing, brethren beloved by God, His choice of you . . .

P: 1 Thessalonians 5:9: For God has not destined us for wrath, but for obtaining salvation through our Lord Jesus Christ.

P, E: 1 Thessalonians 5:24: Faithful is He who calls you, and He also will bring it to pass.

P, E: 2 Thessalonians 2:13: God has chosen you from the beginning for salvation through sanctification by the Spirit and faith in the truth.

E: 1 Timothy 1:1: Paul an apostle of Christ Jesus according to the command of God our Savior . . .

1 Timothy 1:13-14: Even though I was formerly a blasphemer and a persecutor and a violent aggressor. And yet I was shown mercy, because I acted ignorantly in unbelief; and the grace of our Lord was more

than abundant, with the faith and love which are found in Christ Jesus. [Ed., If the prerequisite for mercy is ignorance and unbelief, then who will fail to qualify? Also, note that both faith and love are found only in Christ. Not until we find Christ, or more correctly, only when He finds us, do we find faith and real love.]

1 Timothy 2:4: Who desires ["who will have," KJV] all men to be saved and to come to the knowledge of the truth.

E: 1 Timothy 4:10: For it is this we labor and strive, because we have fixed our hope on the living God, who is the Savior of all men, especially [Greek, *malista:* most of all] of believers.

2 Timothy 1:1: Paul, an apostle of Christ Jesus by the will of God . . .

P, E: 2 Timothy 1:9: Who has saved us, and called us with a holy calling, not according to our works, but according to His own purpose and grace which was granted us in Christ Jesus from all eternity.

2 Timothy 2:25-26: With gentleness correcting those who are in opposition, if perhaps God may grant them repentance leading to the knowledge of the truth, and they may come to their senses [Ed., see the Prodigal Son story, lit. "he came to himself" (Luke 15:17)] and escape from the snare of the devil, having been held captive by him to do his will.

P: 2 Timothy 4:18: The Lord will deliver me from every evil deed, and will bring me safely to His heavenly kingdom; to Him be the glory forever and ever. Amen.

E: Titus 1:1: Paul, a bond-servant of God, and an apostle of Jesus Christ, for the faith of those chosen of God . . .

Titus 2:11: For the grace of God has appeared, bringing salvation to all men.

Titus 3:5: He saved us, not on the basis of deeds which we have done in righteousness, but according to His mercy . . .

Hebrews 2:8: Thou hast put all things in subjection under His feet. For in subjecting all things to Him, He left nothing that is not subject to Him.

Hebrews 2:9: That by the grace of God He might taste death for every one.

Hebrews 2:10: For it was fitting for Him, for whom are all things, and through whom are all things, in bringing many sons to glory, to perfect the author of their salvation through sufferings.

P, E: Hebrews 6:17: In the same way God, desiring even more to show to the heirs of the promise the unchangeableness of His purpose, interposed with an oath.

P: Hebrews 8:8-12: "Behold days are coming," says the Lord, "when I will effect a new covenant . . . I will put my laws into their minds, and I will write them on their hearts. And I will be their God, and they shall be My people . . . for all shall know Me, from the least to the greatest of them. For I will be merciful to their iniquities, and I will remember their sins no more." [Ed., The new covenant prophesied by Jeremiah.]

Hebrews 9:26: Otherwise, He would have needed to suffer often since the foundation of the world; but now once at the completion of the ages He has been manifested to put away sin by the sacrifice of Himself.

Hebrews 12:2: Fixing our eyes on Jesus, the author and finisher of our faith . . .

James 1:18: In the exercise of His will He brought us forth by the word of truth, so that we might be, as it were, the first fruits among His creatures.

James 2:13: Mercy triumphs over judgment.

E: 1 Peter 1:1: Peter . . . to those . . . who are chosen according to the foreknowledge of God the Father . . .

P, E: 1 Peter 1:3: Blessed be the God and Father of our Lord Jesus Christ, who according to His great mercy has caused us to be born again to a living hope through the resurrection of Jesus Christ from the dead, to an inheritance which is imperishable and undefiled and will not fade away, reserved in heaven for you.

1 Peter1:20-21: For He was foreknown before the foundation of the world, but has appeared in these last times for the sake of you who through Him are believers in God.

E: 1 Peter 2:9: But you are a chosen race, a royal priesthood, a holy nation, a people for God's own possession, that you may proclaim the excellencies of Him who has called you out of darkness into His marvelous light.

E: 1 Peter 3:9: For you were called for the very purpose that you might inherit a blessing.

1 Peter 3:18: For Christ also died for sins once for all, the just for the unjust, in order that He might bring us to God, having been put to death in the flesh, but made alive in the spirit.

1 Peter 4:6: For the gospel has for this purpose been preached even to those who are dead [i.e., the disobedient spirits in prison from the days of Noah (Pet 3:18-20)], that though they are judged in the flesh as men, they may live in the spirit according to the will of God.

P, E: 1 Peter 5:10: And after you have suffered for a little, the God of all grace, who called you to His eternal glory in Christ, will Himself perfect, confirm, strengthen and establish you.

1 Peter 5:12: I have written to you briefly, exhorting and testifying that this is the true grace of God. Stand firm in it!

E: 2 Peter 1:10: Therefore, brethren, be all the more diligent to make certain about His calling and choosing you.

2 Peter 3:9: The Lord is not slow about His promise, as some count slowness, but is patient toward you, not purposing [Greek, *boulema:* resolving (Ed., as opposed to wishing or desiring)] for any to perish but for all to come to repentance.

1 John 4:14: And we have beheld and bear witness that the Father has sent the Son to be the Savior of the world.

E: Jude 1:1: Jude, a bond-servant of Jesus Christ, and brother of James, to those who are called, beloved in God the Father, and kept for Jesus Christ.

Jude 1:24: Now to Him who is able to keep you from stumbling, and to make you stand in the presence of His glory blameless with great joy . . .

Revelation 1:17-18: I am the first and the last, and the living One; and I was dead, and behold, I am alive forevermore, and I have the keys of death and of Hades.

Revelation 5:13: And every created thing [Greek: every creature] which is in heaven and on the earth and under the earth and on the sea, and all things in them, I heard saying [i.e., worshiping], "To Him who sits on the throne, and to the Lamb, be blessing and honor and glory and dominion forever and ever."

P, E: Revelation 13:8: And all who dwell on the earth will worship him [the beast], every one whose name has not been written in the book of life of the Lamb who was slain from the foundation of the world.

P: Revelation 15:3-4: Great and marvelous are Thy works, O Lord God, the Almighty; Righteous and true are Thy ways, Thou King of the nations. Who will not fear, O Lord, and glorify Thy name? [Ed., The answer implied is "none."] For Thou alone art holy; for all the nations will come and worship before Thee, for Thy righteous acts have been revealed.

P, E: Revelation 17:14: And those who are with Him are the called and chosen and faithful.

P: Revelation 17:17: For God has put it in their hearts to execute His purpose by having a common purpose, and by giving their kingdom to the beast, until the words of God should be fulfilled.

P: Revelation 22:13: I am the Alpha and the Omega, the first and the last, the beginning and the end.

[Editorial note by David Sprenger: An attempt has been made to include the most prominent scriptures concerning the sovereignty of God over all His creation. More are being added as they are discovered. There are also many others too numerous to mention which were not included because of repetition or the close similarity with those already listed.]

Appendix B

---**❧**---

Flowchart

NOTE: Appendix B is a Color Graphic Available at
www.SoWhyDidntTheyTellMeThatInChurch.com

APPENDIX C

PARADOX GRAPHIC

NOTE: THIS CHART CAN BE VIEWED IN COLOR AT
www.SoWhyDidntTheyTellMeThatInChurch.com

The Paradox

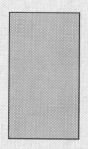 +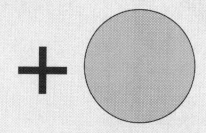

This rectangle represents the idea that GOD IS SOVEREIGNLY IN CONTROL OF EVERYTHING.

This circle represents the idea that MAN HAS VOLITION and is RESPONSIBLE FOR HIS DECISIONS.

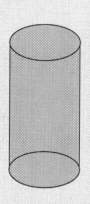

This cylinder represents *The* Paradox of BOTH TRUTHS IN ONE.

APPENDIX D

CASE STUDY/ANALOGY: JONATHAN AND SCOTT

The following fictional case study helps to show why God must have been in charge of seemingly insignificant, as well as major events, in the past in order for things to be in place today.

In 1509 a young man named Jonathan fled London as another plague was beginning to devastate the city. He walked toward Bedfordshire, about fifty miles north, where he came to a fork in the road and for no particular reason decided to go left rather than right. As evening approached, it looked like rain. He saw a farmhouse and decided to ask the owner if he could sleep in the small outbuilding for the night. Early the next morning the old farmer came out to ask Jonathan if he would be interested in a job helping him with his crops and animals. He gladly embraced the opportunity.

A couple of months later the farmer learned that a young couple who owned a small dairy about a mile away had been attacked the night before, The young wife had been raped and her husband murdered. Jonathan's employer and his wife went to see the young widow three to four times a week to help her and to see how she was doing.

Jonathan went along often, and over a few months, he and the young widow became interested in each other and eventually married, remaining together for many years. They had five children, including the son who was conceived the night of the rape. That son married and also had children and grandchildren.

Ten generations later, Scott was born. He joined the British military in 1775 and found himself the next year fighting the Continental Army in New England. In one battle a sniper shot a .50 caliber lead ball at Scott, the very instant his horse tripped—crushing Scott's leg. He survived the battle and was taken to an infirmary where a young

Hessian nurse took care of him. They fell in love and eventually had a daughter.

Four generations later your grandfather was born.

Consider these details, asking yourself whether you would be here today if any of these had been different:

1) If Jonathan had made a right turn, instead of a left in 1509.
2) If the weather had not looked bad that night, causing Jonathan to stop at the farmer's house.
3) If the marauders had not murdered the young farmer and raped his wife.
4) Consider the hundreds of other situations that had to take place in order for all the people to marry and have children at the right times and places so that Scott would eventually be born.
5) If the sniper had pulled his trigger one second earlier.
6) If the young Hessian nurse had not been assigned to take care of Scott when there were many other injured soldiers.
7) Consider all the trivial details as well as the major events that had to occur in order for your grandfather to have been born.
8) Most of us reading this scenario should consider that we might not be here if the world had not been thrown into the turmoil of World War II. What if Hitler had not somehow turned Europe upside down? Would you have met your spouse? Would your parents or grandparents have been where they were?

Psalm 139:16 (NLT): "You saw me before I was born. Every day of my life was recorded in Your book. Every moment was laid out before a single day had passed."

Galatians 1:15 (NLT): "But even before I was born, God chose me and called me by His marvelous grace. Then it pleased Him . . ."

Psalm 119:73: "Your hands have made and fashioned me; give me understanding that I may learn Your commandments."

Job 10:8 (NLT): "You formed me with Your hands; You made me, yet now You completely destroy me."

Acts 17:26: "And He made from one man every nation of mankind to live on all the face of the earth, having determined allotted periods and the boundaries of their dwelling place."

Job 9:22 (NLT): "Innocent or wicked, it is all the same to God. That's why I say, 'He destroys both the blameless and the wicked.'"

Psalm 56:8 (NLT): "You keep track of all my sorrows. You have collected all my tears in Your bottle. You have recorded each one in Your book."

1 Samuel 2:7: "The LORD makes poor and makes rich; He brings low and He exalts."

Ephesians 1:11: "In Him we were also chosen, having been predestined according to the plan of Him who works out everything in conformity with the purpose of His will."

Isaiah 25:1 (NLT): "O LORD, I will honor and praise Your name, for You are my God. You do such wonderful things! You planned them long ago, and now You have accomplished them."

Proverbs 16:33 (NLT): "We may throw the dice, but the LORD determines how they fall."

Proverbs 20:24: "A man's steps are from the LORD; how then can man understand His way?"

Daniel 2:21: "He changes times and seasons; he removes kings and sets up kings; he gives wisdom to the wise and knowledge to those who have understanding.

APPENDIX E

LIST OF SOME WELL-KNOWN CONDITIONALISTS

1) F. F. Bruce—Professor of New Testament & Exegesis, Manchester University. Respectfully was known as "The Dean of New Testament Commentaries."

2) John Stott—Cleric, scholar, author, well-respected theologian. Billy Graham called him one of the greatest voices of Christianity. *Time* magazine's top 100 most influential people.

3) Michael Green—Scholar, author.

4) E. Earle Ellis—Biblical scholar. Research Professor of Theology Emeritus at Southwestern Baptist Theological Seminary in Fort Worth.

5) Edward Fudge—Pastor, author, researcher, attorney. *The Fire That Consumes* is considered by many to be the most thorough treatise on conditional immortality written in our time.

6) Philip E. Hughes—Theologian and guest professor at Westminster Theological Seminary and Reformed Theological Seminary.

7) Richard Bauckham—Widely published scholar in historical theology and New Testament. Sr. Scholar at Ridley Hall Cambridge. Author.

8) Thomas H. Olbricht—Harvard Divinity. Minister, prolific author, renowned scholar, Professor Emeritus Pepperdine University.

9) John McRay—Wheaton College Graduate School. Well published in archeology and Pauline studies.

10) John Stackhouse, Jr.—Journalist, scholar, author. Holds position formerly held by J.I. Packer at Regent College.

11) Dale Moody—Author and professor of theology for nearly forty years, Southern Baptist Theological Seminary.

12) John Franke—Biblical Seminary, Hatfield, Pennsylvania. Doctorate in Philosophy, Oxford.
13) Homer Hailey—Author of fifteen theological books. Professor at Abilene Christian and Florida College.
14) Thomas L. Robinson—Union Theological Seminary, Princeton Theological Seminary, Harvard, Pepperdine, Abilene Christian.
15) Clark Pinnock—Well-known theologian, apologist, author. McMaster University, New Orleans Baptist Theological Seminary, Trinity Divinity School.
16) John Wenham—New Testament Greek scholar, conservative Anglican theologian, author.
17) Oscar Cullman—New Testament scholar, University of Strasbourg; author, apologist, member Academie des Siences.
18) Edward White—Minister, theologian, author.

Appendix F

Verses In Chapter 10
(Biblical Order)

( ) INDICATES THE ORDER WITHIN THE CHAPTER

Genesis 2:17 (16)
Genesis 3:19 (3)
Exodus 12:24 (43)
Exodus 21:6 (42n)
Exodus 40:15 (44)
Deuteronomy 15:17 (40)
Deuteronomy 23:3 (42n)
I Samuel 1:22,28 (39)
I Samuel 27:12 (41)
Job 12:10 (47)
Psalm 1:6 (66)
Psalm 21:9 (4)
Psalm 30:5 (17)
Psalm 37:1,2 (30)
Psalm 37:20 (31)
Psalm 37:38 (32)
Psalm 49:20 (62)
Psalm 68:2 (67)
Psalm 92:7 (14)
Psalm 103:9 (17)
Psalm 112:10 (34)
Psalm 146:4 (65)
Proverbs 11:19 (24)
Ecclesiastes 9:5 (68)
Isaiah 13:9 (74)